Early Praise for *Set Up*

"*Set Up* is an outstanding tool to help leaders at all levels be successful. You can see Mark Noon's teambuilding expertise. He has a way of relating storytelling with proven leadership, and his personal experiences bring the concepts of leadership to life. His passion for leadership excellence is presented throughout the book.

Competition is tough, and Mark gives us tools for leaders to prepare your entire organization for success. This book is clear and concise to take any organization from good to great!"
—Jean Anthony, president and CEO of Hills & Dales General Hospital

"Mark is a master at connecting people to purpose and value. He coaches and teaches how to create the highest value in leaders and for leaders to create the highest engagement in work and life. This book was published in a few months but took a lifetime to create. Mark leads with conviction and will show you how to do the same. Creating the setting is the foundation of how your culture will be lived out, and the legacy of your life and organization will be built by the stories you tell. You will enjoy reading every chapter, and your life will be different when you take to heart each element cover to cover."
—Steve Vaggalis, lead pastor of Destiny Worship Center

"This book has the life and leadership lessons to make you better at what you do, no matter what that is. Mark is my colleague, but even better, he is my friend. I know what makes him tick, and his calling truly is to make others better. I always gauge a book by how I 'hear' the voice of the author, and I 'hear' Mark here loud and clear. The stories and concepts written in this book are timeless, motivating, encouraging, and will lift you to greater heights in all that matters to you. The lessons learned will propel you to do better, be better, and will set you up to be the success you desire to be. Read it cover to cover and then read it again. You will not be disappointed."
—Rich Bluni, RN, Studer Group senior leader, national speaker, and author of *Inspired Nurse, Oh No…Not More of That Fluffy Stuff!*, and *Inspired Nurse Too*

"Mark Noon has a way of connecting with people through storytelling from the stage. His humor and real-life leadership challenges are easy for audiences to relate to, and the accessible leadership applications he shares offer audiences valuable takeaways.

Readers who are ready to take their leadership skills to the next level will value this book. From building relationships and aligning department culture with organizational values to developing employees with coaching and recognition to empower engagement, *Set Up* is a great mentoring resource for the leadership toolbox.

As a friend and colleague, I know the content on the pages of Mark's book will benefit the aspiring leader. The discipline of his military background, his healthcare leadership experience, and the compassionate heart of this family man bring leadership solutions to life."
—Kris Ann Piazza, Studer Group coach

SETUP

TIMELESS LEADERSHIP SKILLS
FOR YOUR SUCCESS

MARK A. NOON

Published by:
Studer Group
350 West Cedar Street
Suite 300
Pensacola, FL 32502
Phone: 866-354-3473
Fax: 850-332-5117
www.publishing.studergroup.com

ISBN: 978-1-62218-102-5

Library of Congress Control Number: 2018949109

The stories in this book are true. However, some names and identifying details have been changed to protect the privacy of all concerned.

Printed in the United States of America

Dedication

To the most extraordinary, exceptional woman – my wife, Michelle – who has set up our family to be the very best we can be. I cannot imagine life without you. You continue to be my very best friend and the love of my life. I cherish you.

To my kids, Taylor, Hannah, Bailey, and Keenan, undoubtedly the most important people I have worked to set up in life. You are my inspiration to keep doing what is right and good.

Thanks be to my God Most High and my savior, Jesus. I am so blessed.

Table of Contents

Introduction

On July 28, 2000, I moved from Staff Sergeant Mark Noon, United States Air Force to Second Lieutenant Mark Noon, in an official promotion ceremony. I was promoted because I was a good laboratory technician, or laboratory scientist as we know them today. This wasn't necessarily the wrong way of identifying a new leader, but was it the best way? What preparation or training had I received that qualified me for promotion to a leadership position? I had a weekend to think about it. After that, I was supposed to be ready to lead, to engage, to do *something*. But what on earth was I supposed to do?

This very question is the reason why I have dedicated the past 15+ years to learning about and teaching leader development. We put people in a position to fail by not preparing them as best we can for leadership. The inaccurate assumption that leadership skills are either innate or easily learned is why this book is so vital. According to a 2011 CareerBuilder survey, more than a quarter of the surveyed managers said they were not ready to become a leader when they started managing others, and 58% said they didn't receive any management training.[1] Another survey indicated that more than 80% of new leaders were not prepared to lead when they first got the job.[2] Is leader development essential? The answer is a resounding "Yes!"

I once read a curious poem, if even a poem at all, by D. H. Lawrence: "I have never seen a wild thing sorry for itself. A small bird will drop frozen dead from a bough without ever having felt sorry for itself." Think about this: wild animals do not feel sorry for themselves, but many human beings will wallow in self-pity, selfishly unaware of their action's impact on their goals and dreams. Those that want to be leaders, or are currently leading, will instead seek mentors and opportunities to change their circumstances, just as a wild animal will shrug off obstacles and persevere through adversity.

Several years ago, my oldest daughter, Hannah, began playing volleyball, followed shortly thereafter by my younger daughter, Bailey. Since that time, I've grown to love the game. As I learned the sport and began to analyze it, I found so many correlations to business/non-profit work, management and leadership, and even to parenting. Each player has a unique function, position, and responsibility. If everyone in the organization does what they're supposed to do, then every team player, every member makes that organization successful.

In volleyball there are six different positions on the court: the outside hitter, opposite hitter (also called right side), the middle blocker, defensive specialist, a libero (a kind of defensive specialist), and the setter. If you have never watched a volleyball match, you could compare the setter to the quarterback of a football team. In many ways, the setter does not receive the kind of attention that the hitters may receive, whereas the quarterback is usually the highlighted person on the offense, but they are vital to the success of the team.

One day as I was watching my daughters play, it struck me how the setter is the catalyst for the rest of the team. I realized that the entire operation of a volleyball match is to create a set up for the hitters score a point, which makes the setter absolutely essential. In that moment, I lost track of the game and began to ponder the role I've played in each of my many teams. Did I create the set up? Did I set up people in the right position? Did I set up my team with the right information? Did I set up myself for success? Did I set up others for success?

This is a book about leadership essentials. It is about truth, and all truth is confrontational. It takes courage to hear the truth, and courage to make a change. It is written in a manner that is easy to understand, easy to relate to, and easy to put into practice. There is no doubt whether you're a corporate CEO, quarterback on a football team, a brand new entry-level employee, or a manager in any field – this book is for you. It will take you step by step and prepare you for leadership. Better yet, it will help you to step into leadership.

My will shall shape the future. Whether I fail or succeed shall be no man's doing but my own. I am the force; I can clear any obstacle before me or I can be lost in the maze. My choice; my responsibility; win or lose only I hold the key to my destiny.

– Elaine Maxwell

1

Getting Directions:
Finding Out Who You Are,
Where You Are Going,
And How to Get There

When Hannah was ten years old, I bought her a tetherball set. She fell in love with hitting the ball. She played for hours a day during that summer. When she entered middle school, a friend invited her to play volleyball on the 6th grade team. She was hooked. In time, volleyball helped provide direction and goals for her life. She worked and trained as a setter with the intention of receiving a volleyball scholarship for college, and after six years of barriers and victories those goals were achieved. Over time, her passion set the course for her sister, Bailey, to follow in her footsteps. What a blessing, to have both girls' college tuitions paid for. Even my goals were accomplished.

I remember Christmas morning as a child being a tremendous time of excitement. Santa Claus left the most amazing toys under the tree. The new bike was already set up. I could immediately get on the bike and ride around the neighborhood, not wasting any time (Ok, I lived in Michigan's Upper Peninsula, so maybe riding around the block was not happening because of the snow and cold). The train already had batteries in it, set up on the track, prepared to go for hours of fun.

How different it was when I became a parent. Little did I realize as a child, that bicycle came with directions. Somebody had to put it together! As an adult, how many Christmas Eves have you spent putting together a bicycle or some other toy? If you're like me, you probably didn't think you needed directions. I have put together countless projects over the years: bookcases, bicycles, television cabinets, model cars, and that first volleyball net in the backyard. Each item came with instructions specifically designed to teach me how to assemble it. I remember putting together a TV cabinet once. I thought to myself, "This is simple. There is a right side and there's a left side." I didn't bother to pay attention to the pieces marked A, B, or C. I got all the way to the end of the project, ready to put the final doors on this cabinet. And what should I find? The doors were on the wrong side. I had to take it apart and put it back together using the directions.

Why is it we think we don't want, use, or ask for directions? We'll pull out a map or Global Positioning System, search the internet, look at the sun and stars, check the wind's direction, but we don't ask for help. We even question the GPS and don't believe the instructions given. These are proven sources of direction and yet we choose, at times, not to heed them. Okay, so it's not quite like that all the time, but if I learned one thing over the years it is this: I need help.

My dad spent 60+ years driving a semi-truck. As a kid, I spent quite a few miles in the sleeper cabin while traveling the country with him. My dad has an amazing recall for directions. When I travel, I will tell him where I am going, and he will name the roads I need to take and restaurants that are along the way. He even has people call him to ask directions when they are across the country. People look to him for direction. He has my best interest at heart and his directions are very accurate. Why would I not follow them? In the end, it's all about trust.

Fortunately, I learned that lesson early on. I need trustworthy people, their direction, and their partnership; so does everyone else. Even though we get frustrated with being lost, we have so many means to gain directions. To say "no man is an island" is to understate the principle of teamwork. To understand the principles by which this book is written, it is important to be humble and to seek help and guidance. Great leaders know that humility leads to learning, expertise and, finally, results. But without the help of others, even the most humble person is at a disadvantage. It is important to realize that we need each other.

Selflessness and Selfishness

As a manager in a business, or as a coach with a team, you not only need direction for your own life, you need to know how to give direction. To be fully effective in whatever you do in life, you need to know what direction you are going. If you don't know where you're going, how can you show someone else the way?

The definition of selfless is "Having little or no concern for one's self." So, what's wrong with being selfless? Nothing, except most of us have a little bit in us that I call WIIFM, or "What's In It For Me." Is that wrong? Yes, regarding fame, position, etc. But to get direction for your life, you need to be *selfish* at first. Let me say that again – even though your motivation may be to help others, even though we feel the need inside to do what's right for others – **before we concern ourselves with others, we must think about ourselves.** To give direction to others we should first have direction for ourselves. My friend and colleague, Rich Bluni, compares this to being on a flight that's in distress. On any given flight, the crew will instruct you to place an oxygen mask over your own mouth, before you attempt to help anyone else, including those more vulnerable. By doing so, you ensure that you can assist almost anyone within reach, because you have what you need to sustain yourself. Be selfish, internally, to be the best and brightest you can be.

All of us have different directions or things we want and need to do in life. The starting line of life is not equal; everyone has their own unique set of circumstances. Some start out in business with a high school education. Others have college experience and advanced degrees. Some have parents who taught them well. Some did not. No matter our circumstances, we can all get to the same goal, though our roads may be different. This is where you pull out the roadmap and say to yourself, "Where is it that I want to travel? What is it I want to do with my life, with my business, or my team? What do I want to accomplish most in life?" Fulfilling the answers to these questions, which can take a lifetime, helps you to reach your goals and to set up others for success along the way.

I also truly believe that God will bring people into your life who have been where you want to go, to help create a path to get you there. People rarely improve unless they have someone to look up to. It's possible, though, with enough grit and determination.

But, I've seen what a difference it makes to have others invest and mentor those who come after them. If you rate yourself as a 6 on a scale of 1-10, then you had better start hanging around others who you feel are a 7 and above. As T. Harv Eker explains in his book, *Secrets of the Millionaire Mind,* "Successful people look at other successful people as a means to motivate themselves. They see other successful people as models to learn from. They say to themselves, 'If they can do it, I can do it.'"[1] Some years after I had become an officer in the US Air Force, I found out that my journey had inspired (at the time) at least 11 others in the Air Force to finish their degrees and apply for an officer commission as I had done. I also found out that the reason for several of them was, "If Mark can do it, so can I." I'm sure what they really meant was, "If Mark can, anyone can."

Find inspiration from others, find out their secret, and you will find direction and success.

Purpose

Purpose. Worthwhile work. Making a difference. Those three tenets were taught to me during my first week working for Studer Group. They are the very center – the *why* – of what we do. After spending 20 years in the United States Air Force, the last five years within that timeframe teaching the very principles Studer Group® coaches, I was able to join this illustrious group. And even though I taught the Why Principle – how what we do needs to be focused around our purpose – I still didn't fully grasp the meaning for many years.

Simon Sinek's TED Talk on the psychological and physiological aspects of understanding the why hit me like a ton of bricks. It also appealed to my analytical and scientific brain. In it, he said, "Every single person and organization on the planet knows what they do. Some know how they do it, whether you call it your differentiating proposition or proprietary process or USP. But very few people and organizations know why they do what they do. And by why I don't mean to make a profit; that's a result. By why I mean, what's your purpose? What's your cause? What's your belief? Why does your organization exist?"[2]

I use some of these concepts when I speak to an audience to link them to why I'm there, and the why of the message. Even more importantly, I share the why to help leaders communicate with their teams, colleagues, and customers. Why matters; I cannot overstate this point. It matters emotionally and physically.

Sinek goes on, "If you look at a cross-section of the human brain, looking from the top down, what you see is that the human brain is actually broken into three major components that correlate perfectly with the Golden Circle. Our newest brain – our homo sapien brain, our neocortex – corresponds with the "what" level. The neocortex is responsible for all rational, analytical thought, and language. The middle two sections make up our limbic brain which is responsible for all of our feelings, like trust and loyalty. It's also responsible for all human behavior and decision making, and it has no capacity for language. In other words, when we communicate from the outside in, then yes, people can understand vast amounts of complicated information like features, benefits, facts, and figures. It just doesn't drive behavior. When we communicate from the inside out, we are talking directly to the part of the brain that controls behavior and then we allow people to rationalize it with the tangible things we say and do. This is where gut decisions come from."[3] Literally, the brain is centered around the why. It's how we were created. Connecting to it is only natural.

In addition, *Harvard Business Review* featured a breakthrough article in January 2017 which discussed the emotional and physiological response to the why. In "The Neuroscience of Trust", Paul J. Zak articulates, based on the experiments he had conducted, eight ways that leaders can effectively create and manage a culture of trust. "Trust creates joy, and joy on the job comes from doing purpose-driven work. When an employee experiences a moment of trust, oxytocin is released deep within the recesses of the brain."[4] Zak continues, "I hypothesize that there must be a neurological signal that indicates when we should trust someone. Oxytocin released from the brain appeared to do just one thing – reduce the fear of trusting someone."[5] Incidentally, oxytocin is also called the "love hormone" or "cuddle hormone". So, when we trust someone we don't necessarily love them, but we bond with them in a way. We connect. And when we connect we can relate, and if we can relate we can accomplish great and mighty things.

Connecting to the why creates purpose. When you understand the purpose of why you do something, the how and the what are easy to digest. When you're able to connect people to the why and they understand its purpose, they trust you. Leaders are going to be trusted when they help people connect to purpose. What is your purpose? Where do you find purpose? Is it in your work? Is it in your church? Is it in your family? It can certainly be in all these areas.

I once visited the Billy Graham Library in Charlotte, North Carolina. Billy Graham has always been a hero to me (and a great loss, as he passed on during the writing of this book). He was a man that God used to change the world. While taking a tour of the library, I watched several taped interviews of Reverend Graham over the years. In one of the interviews, he talked about his purpose. He said several presidents had asked him to be an ambassador to other nations. He said no to every one of them. When asked why he said no, Rev. Graham said he knew his purpose was to serve God, not presidents. How many of us would turn down such a great honor? Billy Graham did, because he understood his why.

So, to recap, the first step in understanding and getting direction is to understand purpose. If your life is organized around a purpose it is more productive, it is clearly expressed, and well-defined. You cannot be fulfilled if you do not have purpose. From purpose we set expectations and goals. In a later chapter, we will discuss why expectations and goals need to be clearly defined.

Once we find purpose we can then define the direction of our lives. Remember, we need to know the purpose of our trip, then we lock in GPS directions to get to our destination.

1. Define the goal.

Define what you want to accomplish and what you want to become. Go ahead, write it down. Effectiveness in whatever it is you want to do is dependent upon a clear definition of the terms. Don't make arbitrary goals, ensure they are distinctive and specific. Anyone should be able to read your list of goals and know exactly what you want to achieve. You should be able to tell anyone your goals in a sentence or two. Just as the vision of any company or organization should be so easy to see, so should your goals.

Your goal may be to win the championship. Define what championship – whether district, regional, or state. The goal may be to be the fastest runner on the Olympic team, but what race? The vision for your company may be to be the best. To be the best at what? When circumstances arise that seem contrary to the result, look back to the definition of what your goal is.

In my work with organizations around the country, I always ask the senior leadership for their vision. The vision, of course, is simply the goal. I've seen some lofty goals. I'm very much in favor of them! Sometimes, we call those BHAGs: Big Hairy Audacious Goals. However big and hairy, they also have to be realistic. The bigger the goal, the more you need to focus. The bigger the goal, the more you need your team. Be bold.

Long-range (ten to twenty-year) goals are equivalent to the milestones or scenic stops along the journey, but to attain them you also must have weekly, monthly, and annual goals. They are your route to the final destination. A 90-Day Plan is the roadmap to success. Put your goals into bite-sized pieces that are attainable in 90 days. If you want to increase your profits by 10% in a year, a 90-day goal would need to account for 3-4% of that growth. As part of my marathon training, I began running 3 miles each day, then 4 miles certain days the next week, 5 the next week, and so on. After 4 months, I was able to run a 13.1-mile race. I have even incorporated 90-Day Plans into my family's routine and encouraged my children to build their own 90-Day Plans. They didn't want to do it at first, but I knew they would learn valuable lessons about how to plan for success. Not only have they embraced the practice, my daughter, Hannah, even used the concept in one of her leadership papers in college, although I think she may have been poking fun at me.

Three times in my life I had a goal to run a marathon. Three times I failed. The first time was due to an injury to my left knee. The other two times I simply quit. This was very frustrating for me because I have been a runner for almost 40 years. Finally, after quitting the third time, I decided to lessen the goal and run a half marathon. I was successful. Do I still desire to run a marathon someday? Absolutely. Sometimes our goals are just bigger than our will. Or, as my parents used to tell me when we would go to a buffet, "Your eyes are bigger than your stomach."

I once worked with a hospital whose vision was to be the number one rural hospital in America. That for sure was a BHAG. It was also unrealistic. There are over 2,000 rural hospitals in America. If you are floating around number 100 out of 2,000, being number one is a bit impractical. What if the vision was to be the number one hospital in their region, then maybe state, and then maybe the country? Setting and attaining the individual, small goals help to build the foundation to get to the Big Hairy Audacious Goal.

Lowering the goal does not make it any less of a success. Making goals realistic will help you accomplish them, and then the bigger goals will become more attainable. The surest, noblest way to fail is to set one's standards monstrously high. The flip side of that proposition also seems true. The surest way to succeed and attain very little is to keep one's striving low. The right balance of goals is necessary. You need to get to the moon before reaching Mars, but don't sell yourself short with goals set too low when your potential is much higher.

Sometimes, you may have to do a reset. You may think you're going to accomplish something and you'll fail. When you hit the reset button on your computer, it restores itself back to its original purpose in performance. It can sometimes take you back to the original. You don't always need to reset all the way back to the beginning, but to the previous level or what was recently saved. It's ok to reset, revise the plan, and go back after the goal.

After running many 10 kilometer races, I finally finished a half marathon. I have goals today to eventually run a marathon or two, and even a triathlon. I also have a goal to compete in a CrossFit competition. I have goals to write four more books in addition to this one.

In my military career, I had a goal to be an officer. At the time, I thought the most logical, most practical route was to be a physician assistant. I took the right classes and prepared for what I thought would be my life's work. I fell short by not getting accepted to the school. So, I did a reset. I finished my laboratory science degree and became an officer and lab director. This actually enabled me to pursue other goals more effectively and brought me to where I am today: an author, speaker, and coach.

Our dreams and goals can drive us to success despite setbacks. Walt Disney didn't give up on his dream after he was fired from his first job at a newspaper or when his first studio went bankrupt. J.K. Rowling wrote the beginning of the Harry Potter series while on welfare, yet she became one of the richest women in the world. She was also rejected by a dozen publishers. Even Donald Trump is in the *Guinness Book of World Records* for having engineered the biggest financial turnaround in history. It's no wonder he didn't give up when others said he would never be president. Each of these people was successful because they had passion and didn't quit on their goal; they rebounded, adjusted, and attacked again.

Chase the Lion author, Mark Batterson, wrote so well, "Are you living your life in a way that is worth telling stories about? Are you running to the roar? When a lion's roar registers in the auditory cortex, the brain sends an immediate message to the body: run away as fast and as far as you can. That's the normal reaction, but lion chasers aren't normal. They don't run away from what they're afraid of; they run toward the roar."[6]

It is well known that the male lion in a pride does not do the hunting. That is left to the female lion, or lioness. But the male lion does, however, send out a tremendous roar and when their prey hear that roar, they run in the opposite direction. In doing so, they run right into the trap of the lionesses waiting on the other side. So, it is essentially safer to run to the roar. Be bold in your goals and run to the roar. Be genuine about what you can and will accomplish.

Define your goals and write them down in the space provided at the end of this chapter. By writing down each step, it becomes a plan. A plan backed by action makes your dream a reality.

2. Set the goal.

Knowing the goal is different from setting the goal. When I start training for a marathon, how I plan to do that is yet to be determined. That's when I have to set the goal. For example: I will run a marathon when I am 52, and I will do it in less than four hours and thirty minutes. A dream written down, with a date, becomes a goal.

The dictionary defines the word "set" as this: to position oneself in such a way as to be ready to start, to be ready, to be in a particular psychological state, usually that of anticipation. It also means a relatively permanent inclination to react in a certain way, or to make ready, suitable, or equip in advance for a particular purpose or for some use or event. "Set" can also refer to putting a seed in the ground.[7]

When you are ready to set the goal for whatever it is in your life you want to become, or want to accomplish, it should be with anticipation. You should be fully ready to participate. When a farmer sets a seed into the ground, they prepare the soil, water the earth, eliminate weeds, and fully anticipate that there is going to be a harvest.

Imagine yourself under absolute perfect conditions. You have all the money you'll ever need. You have the best education. You're the chairman of the board or director of the department. Remove all deficiencies. It is at this moment that you set your goal. Remember, a goal is something you don't already have. Therefore, the goal should be the epitome of the very best you can become or achieve. Imagine what you would like to be, the person you want to be, and begin to live up to that person.

The incredible speaker, Eric Thomas, passionately shares, "If you only have 24 hours in a day, then what you do with that 24 hours will determine your success. I can tell you all about your life if you just write down your 24-hour schedule for me. I can tell you where you're going to be in 5 years, 10 years, if you keep that schedule." Similarly, I heard a wise man, Pastor Steve Vaggalis, once say, "If you don't live by design you live by default." You are the one who must decide what that design is going to be. You must plan, meticulously, in what direction you're going to go. Plant the seed today. Set the goal. It's never too late to be what you might have been. Create the vision of who you want to be, and then live it.

3. Share the goal.

Now that you have written down your goals and prepared yourself to execute them, it's time to share your goals. Sharing your goal unleashes its power. Once it's shared, you've got to tackle it, if for no other reason than being embarrassed if you don't accomplish it. It is said that when Thomas Edison got an idea he would call a press conference, announce his invention, then go back to his workshop and create it. I have done this often in my business and personal life. "As a man thinks in his heart, so is he," it says in Proverbs 23:7. The Bible also says in Luke 6:45, "Out of the abundance of the heart, the mouth speaks." Whether the goal is to run a marathon, complete a CrossFit competition, or take the next leap in developing my skillset, I tell people I will do it to hold myself accountable. As I was planning and writing this book, for example, I talked about it as a certainty, even when it looked like it may never happen. Essentially, I spoke my dreams into reality. I thought it, then I spoke it, and now I'm doing it.

By sharing the goal, you also enlist others to help you succeed. Remember, you need other people. You need partners. When I first shared my book with close friends and colleagues, I was partnering, sharing my goal, my dream. They helped me get it off the ground, and here we are. When I coach organizations about goal setting, I require every department to share their goals with the rest of the company. Why? When you vulnerably share your desires and allow others to see your passion, it is inevitable that they will want to support you to achieve it. Try it! You'll be amazed by how many people will invest in your goal with their own time, efforts, or ideas. When your purpose becomes more and more attractive, it attracts others to you. You don't have to pursue that which you can attract. We can help each other get to our goals.

Lately, I have been running with a friend each weekend. It helps me train for my next race and he gets someone to push him a little harder for his next race. We have different goals, but we help each other by knowing what we each desire. I run the first 5 or 6 miles of his 10-mile run. He's invested in my goals, and I'm invested in his (at least half of his, mathematically speaking).

Robert Jarvik, who invented the artificial heart, said, "Leaders are visionaries with a poorly developed sense of fear and no concept of the odds against them." Don't be afraid to share your vision. Many people laughed when Bill Gates announced to the world that his goal was to have a computer in every home in America. No one is laughing now. Most of us can't imagine our lives without one! Igor Sikorsky, the inventor of the helicopter, was creating and inventing in the early days of the Wright brothers. People told him human flight was not possible. He is known to have said to his detractors, "The bumblebee cannot fly because of the shape and weight of its body in relation to its wings. The bumblebee does not know this."

In the next chapter we will dive into the top four characteristics of highly effective leaders, but I want to talk about one of those now. Without giving away too much, one of the top traits of leaders which leads to off the chart employee engagement is setting clear goals and expectations. Expectations are typically the standards by which we conduct ourselves, and the goals, of course, are the vision of the organization or person. *Purpose-oriented* people know that the organization has goals, but *purpose-driven* people are focused on those goals, innovate by bringing new ideas, and drive outcomes to the highest level. ***Purpose-oriented* people know the values of the organization; the *purpose-driven* people live them.**

Post your organization's goals in your department, office, or team room. Talk about the goals in department and individual meetings. When rounding (short-but-frequent check-in conversations with each employee), ask your staff or team to articulate to you the goals of the organization and how their work is incorporated into accomplishing those goals. If you have created a compelling vision (goal) for your department or organization and discussed it thoroughly, any time you walk into a department, an employee should see you and think right away, "They're not going to stump me this time! I know our vision!"

1. Write your goal(s), personal and professional.

_____

_____

_____

_____

2. Set your individual, and specific, goals and steps (90-Day Plan).

_____

_____

_____

_____

_____

3. Share your goals, with whom, how, and when.

_____

_____

_____

_____

_____

He has achieved success who has lived well, laughed often and loved much; who has gained the respect of intelligent men and the love of little children; who has filled his niche and accomplished his task; who has left the world better than he found it, whether by an improved poppy, a perfect poem, or a rescued soul; who has never lacked appreciation of Earth's beauty or failed to express it; who has always looked for the best in others and given them the best he had; whose life was an inspiration whose memory a benediction.

– Bessie Stanley

2

The Setter:
A Great Setter Can Make
Everyone Look Great

She stood at the net waiting for the next play. She made certain signs with her hands, seemed to play with her shirt, and then she held up a couple fingers behind her back so only her teammates could see them. The ball came over the net, the libero made a perfect pass. She had her feet in position, her hands went up in the air, and like an eagle soaring through the air she set the ball. The hitter was already on the approach, high in the air she jumped. SMACK! The ball was hit with such force and landed on the floor on the other side. Point, side out. The setter called the play and the team responded.

I love to watch the game of volleyball. The intensity of each play and the intricate movements of each player cause excitement and tension at the same time. I have been to big tournaments in arenas with over 100 courts and 200 teams playing at one time; it can be chaotic, to be sure. If you've never had the opportunity to watch a game of volleyball, I encourage you to do so. I've found a host of correlations as to how teams operate in the sports world and how organizations function.

The Setter Is the Leader

The setter must be a team-first player and cannot play favorites or choose who she sets to, based on anything other than what will benefit the team. The setter must work with a coach to determine the best plays to run, when to run them, and what adjustments should be made. This position does not get a lot of credit for the team's success in the news or sports highlights, but the coach knows that the setter can make the difference between a mediocre team and a great one.

To be a setter, a player should be quick, strong, and decisive. There is no room for doubt in the decisions that a setter makes. She must quickly read the pass, get to the ball, and set the right player at the right time, with the right speed, and the right height of the ball. There is no room for error. There is no time to think things through. Her decisions are made before she ever even touches the ball. If the setter does not know her job, the entire fate of the team can be doomed. The setter must continually strive to improve herself. By position, she is the leader on the floor. She distributes the sets to best help the team and changes the plays based on her teammates' abilities. She makes the team better. Sometimes, that means making decisions that don't please every player.

A setter is a leader. Each time you read the word setter think leader, and vice-versa. Whether you're in an entry-level position or chairman of the board, you can be a leader. A setter motivates and is prepared for whatever comes their way. They accept responsibility and delegate with patience. They analyze their team and look for opportunities to benefit all involved.

As a setter, you hold your team's most influential position and sometimes its most frustrating one. You control the tempo and create the momentum. If you want to lead effectively, you need to be able to make good decisions. If you can learn to do this in a timely and well-considered way, then you can lead your team to spectacular and well-deserved success. However, if you make poor decisions, your team risks failure and your time as a leader may be cut short.

You may not feel very powerful in your present position. But it's not your position in a company or organization that matters, but the role you play. Pablo Picasso once said, "My mother said to me, 'If you become a soldier, you will be a general; if you become a monk, you wind up as the pope.' Instead, I became a painter and wound up as Picasso." Whatever it is you choose to become you will become. And if you choose to set up other people along the way, you will become the best.

This book is designed to help your team, department, company, and (most of all) you. These lessons apply to everyone. Critical thinking allows you to learn from every story, apply every lesson, improve from every tactic, and grow as a leader and person. Stop making excuses and learn from every opportunity. Everyone can be a setter in their organization, regardless of position or title. That's what's so much fun and what's so exciting about this information.

Leading by Example

Albert Einstein said, "Try not to become a man of success but rather try to become a man of value." Adding value or investing in the success of other people is what a setter does – what a leader does. In doing so, you become more valuable as well. The well-respected American philosopher, author, and professor Tom Morris said, "Success is about who you are, not what you have. Successful people work to discover their talents, to develop those talents, and then to use those talents to benefit others as well as themselves."

My early influencers were both United States Air Force colonels, Mike Ward and Walt Kaneakua. Both are now retired from the Air Force and live in Hawaii, which is where I was stationed in the late 90s. Col. Ward is now a professor at a college on Oahu, and Col. Kaneakua has worked with several legislators in Hawaii. I'll forever be indebted to them for the time and effort they invested in my future. As any good setter does, you invest in what you value. They valued me and set me up for a successful Air Force career.

Col. Ward was a clinical laboratory director at one time, just like I was in the Air Force. When I met him, he was the hospital commander (CEO). Col. Ward had all the right connections and wrote a letter of recommendation to become an Air Force officer. He was a mentor as an officer, a Christian man, and a father.

One of the most special moments in my Air Force career was the evening of Col. Ward's retirement dinner. After the pomp and circumstance of a retirement ceremony, Col. Ward began to thank several people and gave gifts to his family and people that were important to him throughout his career. At the very end of his acknowledgements he called me forward and, in front of everyone, proclaimed that I would be an Air Force officer in just a couple months. I had attained the enlisted rank of E5, which is a staff sergeant. This is the same rank he had achieved in 1975 when he was commissioned as an Air Force officer. He wished me the same success he'd achieved and gave me the exact plaque he was given in 1975. It included the enlisted emblems we shared, as well as his own officer ranks, added in over time. It included a quote from Maslow, "What a man can be he must be." I was shocked to see that he had inscribed my name on the plaque in place of his. On the back, he hand-wrote a note to me that said, "I was able to obtain a dream. Now, I pass this plaque and the dream to you. God bless you on the journey!" I retired from the Air Force in 2012 as a major.

While working in the Air Force, Col. Walt Kaneakua would visit the hospital once a month for regular check-ins. At the time, he was the commander of the Hawaii Air National Guard base. His position was a grand responsibility, and each visit Col. Kaneakua would mentor me on different aspects of leadership. I'm not sure that he thought he was mentoring me, but he would share bits of information that helped shape my leadership skills.

I remember one certain visit where he told me that he sometimes worked 80 hours a week. I was shocked, but I'll never forget what he said. Without hesitation, Col. Kaneakua looked straight into my eyes and shared with utmost sincerity, "Mark, that's what you do for your people." In other words, whatever it takes as a leader, it's our responsibility to either do it or make it happen. In later years, I realized that 80 hours per week was probably excessive and maybe the Colonel didn't delegate as many things that he could have. But the lesson remains, "That's what you do for your people."

An organization's culture is a complex thing. It includes the shared history, expectations, written and unwritten rules, values, relationships, and customs that affect everyone's behavior. The setter can influence the culture of an organization to be one that motivates and encourages others. The culture of your organization or the culture of your team is that environment in which you work or play.

Think about it; an organization encounters a problem and the lessons that the people learn from those problems, accurately or otherwise, and how they solve them become the cultural underpinnings of the next generation. Hence, an organization's culture is the sum of the distinctive behaviors, intentions, and values that people develop over time to make sense of the world.

Some might say that leaders don't directly influence organizational outcomes. Rather, they make decisions that shape the culture of the people working in the organization, who in turn influence outcomes. An organization's culture stands between the leader's intentions and the results the organization achieves. Are others encouraged to share their ideas? Do they feel comfortable with their coworkers?

Currently, Amazon sells over 80,000 books about leadership. There's a common theme running through almost all of them; anyone can be a leader. Leadership is not a position. In the words of author John Maxwell, "Leadership is influence, nothing more, nothing less." The setter is a person of influence. It's the person who analyzes the competition and the situation and says, "This is how we can do it," and the rest of the team follows. Every time the setter makes a decision that leads to the team scoring a point, the more influential that person becomes. Or, in the reverse, each time the setter makes a bad decision, the team suffers and may begin to look for another leader.

To truly be a setter, certain core principles must be followed. As I said earlier, you cannot give direction until you have direction. You cannot set up others until you set up yourself. You cannot prepare others until you're prepared. You cannot teach others until you have been taught and have understanding. The setter is a person of integrity with a sincere, deep concern for the mission or the goal. Their vision is so strong others can see it. They are proud of the organization and the team.

Vision

A vision is a statement about what your organization wants to become. It is sometimes inclusive of the goals, or simply the focus of the organization. It should resonate with all members of the organization by helping them feel proud, excited, and part of something bigger than themselves. A vision should stretch the organization's capability and image of itself and give direction to the group's future. Each film on a sports highlight reel almost always shows someone stretching for something. Stretching to reach a ball. Stretching to reach the goal line. A vision statement should stretch an organization or person.

Vision statements range in length from a couple of words to several pages. I highly recommend making shorter vision statements because people will tend to remember a shorter organizational vision. Sometimes you can have a long version of your vision, but then have a shorter catch phrase that people can remember. For instance, "We want to be the best healthcare organization, providing the best service and care for the best patients and customers in the world." The shorter, catchy phrase may be "Providing the best for the best people."

As a lab director, there was not a week that went by that I did not share the vision in my department. The team needs to know constantly what the vision is, so they can attain it. They cannot lose sight of the goal. Encourage others to share their impression and goals within that vision.

Some ways to share the vision:
- Post it on your communication board
- Reference it in one-on-one meetings with employees
- Use it in marketing campaigns
- Use it as screen savers on company computers

What other ideas can you come up with?

_____

_____

_____

_____

_____

Mission

The mission is what the organization is all about. A mission statement defines the company's purpose. The Walt Disney Company's mission is to be one of the world's leading producers and providers of entertainment and information. Walmart's single purpose is to save people money so they can live better. Ken Blanchard, author of _The One Minute Manager_, said, "Connect the dots between individual roles and the goals of the organization. When people see that connection, they get a lot of energy out of work. They feel the importance, dignity, and meaning in their job." The mission statement does that. It connects individuals to the vision.

The mission statement should be a clear, short representation of the project's or group's purpose for existence. I even know people who have their own personal mission statement. Mine is to make an impact on everyone I meet and to create an atmosphere for learning. It should incorporate socially meaningful and measurable criteria addressing conceptions such as the moral or ethical position of the organization, public image, the target market, products and services, the geographic sphere and expectations of growth and profitability. Any employee or team player who is evaluating a strategic decision should first consider the intent of the mission statement.

Pride

As author John Maxwell says, "Fulfilling your mission depends upon lifting the performance of those you lead." Leaders are fair in their actions and careful in their words.

Setters build pride in their team. Setters are not self-promoting. They are comfortable with their position and the authority that goes with it. They don't abuse that authority; they don't take advantage of others. They instill pride and they exude pride.

I once read a story about a General Motors assembly plant in Wilmington, Delaware. In the early 90s this plant was scheduled to close and over 3,500 workers would lose their jobs. General Motors executives said there was nothing that could be done to change the situation. After the executives left, the plant manager, Ralph Harding, made a passionate speech. "There may be nothing we can do to affect this decision. But there is something we can do: we can make them feel really stupid because they are going to shut down the best plant in General Motors!" Harding had a galvanizing vision that brought pride to the organization.

Motivated by his challenge, the employees became newly engaged, working in problem-solving teams with managers to tackle quality control problems and reduce costs. Union leaders and managers worked together more closely than ever to come up with ideas to improve quality and lower costs. Harding kept everyone informed of the plant's progress and vision. Within two years, the workers made that factory the lowest cost producer in General Motors, with the lowest warranty costs as well. Car dealers specifically requested cars manufactured at this plant.

The worker's sense of self-esteem and pride was equal to the financial incentive of keeping their jobs. The payoff of their pride became so clear that General Motors began to institutionalize their processes throughout its other plants.

Pride is many times confused with arrogance, conceit, or self-importance. But pride in a job well done, or great accomplishments of a team, is a source of satisfaction and delight. I was a proud member of the United States Air Force. I think it is the finest military branch in the U.S. and in the world. I am delighted to be have been a part of such an organization, as I am proud of my current employer, Studer Group. I do not think there is a higher performing group of employees anywhere.

Characteristics of a Great Setter

The other aspects of being a great setter, or leader, are the characteristics that should be most ubiquitous. You teach what you know, and you impart who you are.

In an April 2015 Gallup study, Jim Harter and Amy Adkins identified four behavioral characteristics of leaders that engage employees the most, based on feedback from thousands of employees who said they had a great boss:

1. Have regular meetings with their employees — *Rounding*
2. Provide daily communication by phone, email or in person — *Beautiful*
3. Return calls or emails within 24 hours — *Lack of Conversation abt*
4. Have clear goals and expectations[1] — *feedback life & work*

One of the most amazing things that the study points out is that leaders who continuously demonstrate all four behavioral characteristics are 17 times more likely to have an engaged workforce. Conversely, leaders who do not demonstrate any one of those four characteristics are seven times more likely to have disengaged employees.[2]

What does this research mean for you? You help make these behaviors practical for yourself, and for every leader (and up and coming leader) in your organization.

Hold regular meetings. When Studer Group's coaching teams work with organizational leaders, ensuring communication with direct reports is consistent and frequent is a top priority. We call this rounding, or more specifically, Leader Rounding on Employees. It is simply the act of having a monthly proactive conversation, face-to-face, with every employee. In some organizations I have had the pleasure of coaching, I've seen employee engagement improve as much as 20% over a three-year period by using this tactic. Another organization made it to *Modern Healthcare's* Best Places to Work using this method. It's about consistency and accountability, but mostly it's about relationships and trust. If you'd like to learn more about this leadership tactic, visit www.studergroup.com/rounding.

Communicate daily by phone, email or in person. For some, this can seem like a difficult task. Luckily, these days technology allows us to communicate every day and with every employee. Communicate purposefully, not haphazardly or on the fly. This is not the proverbial wave as you enter and exit your office. Schedule time on your calendar to connect daily, just like you would any other appointment, to ensure you are making and keeping these connections with your staff. Great leadership requires dedicated communication from leaders and investment in what matters most to your employees, colleagues, and teammates. This can be a simple message of encouragement. It can also be a thought for the day, personalized for each team member.

Stick to the 24-Hour Rule. You're likely thinking, "How in the world can I return emails and voicemails within 24 hours?" I once felt the same way, but it is possible to adhere to a 24-hour turnaround. I don't always respond with the answer. Often, it's simple acknowledgement that I received the message, that I will get back to them with an answer, and I offer an appropriate timeframe for that answer. This at least allows people to know the message got through. It can be very frustrating for the sender to wonder if their message made it out of "email never-never land."

The great college basketball coach, Pat Summit, once said, "In the absence of feedback, people will always fill in the blanks with a negative." If you don't return a call or an email within 24 or at the most 48 hours, your employees will automatically think negatively things like "my boss doesn't care about me" or "my boss is ignoring me." Think about the last time someone didn't get back to you in a timely manner; what was your reaction?

Set clear goals and expectations. This is the last, and potentially most important, behavioral characteristic of great leaders. Expectations are not a job description. Expectations are the standards by which we conduct ourselves, or how we behave in an organizational setting, such as returning messages within 24 hours, daily communications, etc. The first thing every supervisor, director, manager, and leader should do with a new employee is set clear goals that will be consistently measured, and then align those goals to the expectations or behaviors that are expected in your department.

Whether organizational or personal, goals are necessary for employees to feel valued and appreciated and help move people from purpose-oriented to purpose-driven participants. Purpose-oriented people know what the organization is doing (goals) but their contribution may be minor. Purpose-driven people are focused on the goals, innovate by bringing new ideas, and drive outcomes to the highest level. Remember: Purpose-oriented people know the values of the organization, but purpose-driven people live them.

To really make goals work for the employee and organization, the goals must be measurable. When employees see success around specific goals, it deepens their engagement. They feel appreciated and valued. They work harder. Innovation happens.

The setter is the leader. The setter communicates encouragement, motivation, clear and precise expectations. They are the positive influence and always make an impact. That's who they are even more so than what they do.

What three things are you going to put into place this week, this month?

_____
_____
_____
_____
_____

4 Outcomes of Great Leader

Trust

Care

Communication

Value

Man shapes himself through decisions
that shape his environment.

– Rene Dubos

Culture is not created by accident. It is
shaped by the people who have the
greatest intentions in shaping it.

– Lance Wallnau

3

The Setting:
The Organizational Culture

I observed every player throughout the entire match. Each one knew their part and how they contributed to the team. Each player knew where they had to be on the court. They knew their position. If they forgot or didn't get there on time, the setter would let them know, encourage them, and set them right. The coach had created an atmosphere where every player felt valued. You could sense it on the court; you could sense it in the stands. No one thought they were better than anyone else. No one treated their fellow team members poorly. I sensed that each player knew what the goal was, knew what their part was, and what the team was all about. They had the right setting.

For an organization to be fruitful, it must rest on a solid foundation; just as a tree that bears good fruit has good, solid roots. The fruit at the furthest branch is still connected to the root and receives the same nourishment as those branches near the core. To produce, you must be aligned with the team, the culture, and the organization. Your values must be reflected in the values of the organization, and vice-versa. Whatever you abide in you absorb; meaning, if the culture is a good one, you will absorb good things. The same holds true, unfortunately, for the negative.

Good leaders lead with their people in mind. This means that you must know the people in your department or organization, what they can handle, how they will likely handle it, and how far they can be stretched. An organization's leadership must create a culture that allows employees to feel valued, to feel as though they have ownership, and know that they a part of the team. If you value something, you manage it better. The players and coaches know their part on a sports team. They must know they are valued. Each may get paid differently, but they know how vital they are to the team's success.

If your organization is established and organized correctly, each member of the team knows their part from the first day of onboarding. They know how their role helps the team function as a whole and how the team wins with them. As we will discuss later in this chapter, creating the setting and knowing your role from the beginning is essential to setting people up for victory.

Creating the Setting

According to a study by TARP Worldwide, 50-60% of patients' healthcare dissatisfaction is due to broken policies, procedures, and processes.[1] I would surmise that the same holds true for employees. Often, dissatisfaction stems from broken promises or processes or a lack of trust. If you know you don't have the support of your leadership, it will be evident in all you attempt to do. When employees or players on a team do not have the right equipment or support, they are dissatisfied in their job. It is difficult to function when you make do with what you have, all the while knowing you could do it better or more efficiently with proper tools or equipment. When I coach rounding on employees, I stress that the lack of tools and equipment to do a job is one of the most frustrating things employees deal with. Simple things like not having a printer nearby, requiring employees to walk to another area or department, or out-of-date software that slows computers are low-cost fixes that are seldom considered as causes of turnover.

Corporate culture has little to do with employee benefits, typically. It more likely has to do with the intangible part of the employees' work: how they are treated by their leader and coworkers, the ability to share and explore new ideas, even the way their work environment is maintained. When the company has pride in how it presents itself internally as well as externally, staff members enjoy coming to work. That's the culture. **The culture is simply the customs, traditions, or environment within an organization. It is the setting.**

A setting is the context, environment, or background of a situation. It is the position, direction, or way in which something is set – the state of the environment in which a situation exists. It is the arrangement of scenery or properties that represent a place where you work. It can also be the actual physical position of something. The setting is perfect for the outcome it creates. Think about that for a moment. What outcomes do you have in your organization? The setting created that. What outcomes do you want? The setting will create that.

The setting can be either negative or positive. If you come into an organization that is run by a dictatorial type of leader who rules by power of position, the setting can be toxic, or certainly disengaging. People may feel as though their work is all about the leaders and not about the team. It is the state of that environment, and it can be stifling to the creative nature of team members.

Likewise, the arrangement of scenery or properties can be limiting to those that work in that environment. For instance, if the equipment is arranged in such a manner that makes you take 30 extra steps to complete a task, you would be frustrated or exhausted by the end of the day. By arranging things in a workable manner for those in that area, leaders can improve productivity and reduce stress and illnesses. Having the right tools to do the job will make your organization more productive and lead your team to success. Again, this is all part of the setting. If the leadership is made up of highly stressed individuals, usually they will create a high stress environment. This setting will hinder efficiency.

Stories Build Legends

Think about a group of kids at a campout. It's late in the evening and they're all sitting around a bonfire. Then, one of their chaperones stands up and begins to tell a story. All you can hear are the mysterious sounds of the night, with little visibility beyond their small circle that surrounds the fire. Each child is huddled next to each other, moving closer to the person next to them as the story goes on. It's the perfect setting for a ghost story. The setting is the physical and emotional description of the place in which the story occurs. And by creating this perfect setting, the story becomes more real. This ghost story would not work in the middle of the day, sitting in a cafeteria. The atmosphere of the campout helps the children feel as if they are participating in the story.

Stories build legends, and legends build legacies. The legacy of an organization is the culture that remains even when the originators or founders are no longer there. It's the stories that are told and repeated, that build the legend and legacy of the company. You must share the stories that made your company great. By telling these stories to new hires in particular, you are inviting them into the story, so they can help build it and make the legend greater.

Think about a story of your family or the legacy of a family member. When your elder relatives tell the story, you can almost picture yourself there, especially when they are comparing you to that ancestor. "You look just like your uncle Allan," my family used to tell me. Then my mom would tell me stories of him, and I began to relate more. When he and I would visit together, I would watch him, and think about how much I am like him. My mom created the setting that prepared me to build the legacy of our family.

I'm reminded of the set of a movie, like the one I was on when filming for the movie *Pearl Harbor*. I bet you did not know that I was a famous actor! You have probably seen my face every time you watched that movie since its release in 2001, and never realized you witnessed my few seconds of fame in the scene just before Cuba Gooding, Jr. uses a machine gun to bring down an enemy aircraft.

While stationed with the Air Force in Hawaii in 2000, I had auditioned for the part of a medic on board a ship during the attack on Pearl Harbor. Even though it was a very small part, I had to audition three times, the last audition being in person for the director, Michael Bay. Talk about a nerve-racking interview! My son, Taylor, was also cast in the movie as one of the young boys playing baseball that fateful Sunday morning. He actually has more screen time than I do, spent 5+ hours directly with Michael Bay, and was in the poster announcing the movie in early 2001, but I was paid more, and my name is in the credits.

When I arrived for filming on Ford Island, I was given my own dressing room. I really thought I was something! I dressed in the uniform they provided and awaited my call to the set. When I arrived on board the USS Missouri, which was used as the ship for these scenes, one of the crew members put us in the right spot for the first take. People smeared dirt and fake blood on us to simulate the conditions for the scene. Everything was in place, the cameras were set up, and all the crew members were in their spot. The actors and extras were ready to begin the scene. Everything was in place before Cuba

Gooding, Jr. ever came on the set. It was perfect. So perfect, it only took two takes for us to complete the filming of the scene.

Cuba Gooding, Jr., as a star of the movie, simply had to step in and do his part because everything around him was in order. And every other scene was set up the same way. There was a consistency to what took place and accountability where everyone participated well. After each take, the director and some of the crew reviewed what was filmed. They wanted to see the outcomes right away, to know that the setting was correct. If it wasn't, they would do a retake. Again, the setting is ideal for the outcome it creates. This story has become a legend in our family.

As we've established, the culture of our organization is the setting. But this kind of setting, or culture, is what will bring high reliability and success to every organization. High reliability is about consistency. Each time a patient enters a hospital, they should receive the same experience. A resident at a nursing home should receive the same high level of care from each employee.

Southwest Airlines consistently ranks number one in employee engagement over other airlines.[2] How do they do it? It's well known that Southwest puts their employees first.[3] The reasons why are simple. If you have engaged employees, you will have engaged customers. It boggles my mind why other airlines don't put employees first, instead choosing to put priority on profits or customers. I'm sure you're wondering what's wrong with that, but when you look at Southwest's results, the why is clear. Do you see other airlines ranked in the top 10 or even 20 places to work in the United States? Are those airlines more profitable than Southwest? No. For 43 consecutive years, Southwest Airlines has made money, making it by far the most consistently profitable US carrier.[4]

When I go to hospitals and businesses and I share with them the results Studer Group has cultivated in partner organizations, they have many times made excuses for why they can't or haven't had that type of culture, and therefore those types of results. They have built barriers in their minds or barriers in their culture that's prevented them from being successful. Maybe you have thought or you've heard others in your organization say, "That might work at that other place, but we can't do that here because we're…" Usually the last word of that sentence is *different*. People make excuses to not do what has been proven to work, or what they know is right, because they think they are terminally unique. If it works at Southwest, why won't it work at another airline?

Or, are leaders trying to give employees what they used to need? The culture needs to change to meet the demands of the environment.

I think some organizations thrive on being different; not in a good way that makes them successful, but in a way that gives them an excuse not to step outside their comfort zone. Simply, it's easier. I think it could even be argued that many people or organizations put more energy towards avoiding the things that make for good success, either out of fear of change or unwillingness to do so, than they do towards driving success.

In a story, the characters are set in place, the mood is set, and the anticipation of the end is at hand. Geographically, the setting can be easy, but the best storytellers can draw you in or make you feel as though you are part of the story through the setting. When writing, an author paints a picture with his or her words. Giving some description of the setting will make that picture a more realistic one. It can also be of interest to the reader to see the picture through the eyes of each character.

To better appreciate the stories of Tom Sawyer and Huckleberry Finn, it is important to understand the Mississippi River and the culture of the people that live along that river. Within the pages of that book is the colorful description of its people and places. If you have never traveled along the Mighty Mississippi, you may not understand the vastness of the river or the life along its shores, so the setting plays an important role in the success of the story, the same way setting plays an important part in the success of an organization. The best storytellers draw you in by creating the best setting, just as the best leaders and managers can draw you into an organization by creating the best setting.

When we receive information in bulleted format, like a PowerPoint presentation, we sort this information and discard most of it. But in an organization where a culture of learning has been developed, and storytelling is used to reinforce that culture, our brains react in a different manner. The brain remembers, and our emotions react. So, let me ask you again, what story does your organization have?

To help build a positive culture, you must first build the capacity for others to learn, grow, and thrive. To do that, there are five elements.
1. **Forge Relationships:** If you can't relate you can't connect. If you can't connect, you can't create culture. Work on relationships with others. Make a connection.

2. **Develop Litheness:** Be strong, but flexible and adaptable. Improvise and overcome. Adaptability and flexibility are key to air power, our Air Force leaders would tell us.

3. **Encourage Courage:** Courage does not mean we don't have fear, but in the midst of fear we are relentless in our pursuit.

4. **Allow Risk-Taking:** Support risks by offering them. In addition, offer assistance in the risk.

5. **Enable Empowerment:** Create a culture where people can accomplish great things. You'll find more on this in chapter 10.

Create a Culture

Dr. JoAnne Sujansky, the founder and CEO of KEY group, once said, "Leaders identify and address the needs of employees while helping them to focus on the needs of the business. Companies can create a corporate culture that aligns employees with the corporate vision. They need to create a culture that shares the vision, the big picture, with all employees, and engages them in achieving the vision. Creating a cycle of winning means hiring top-quality people not just for their skills, but for their raw talent, values, and character. We can teach skills, but we may not always successfully imbue others with a work ethic, integrity, or optimism. This requires companies to raise communication with employees to an art form."[5]

Creating the proper setting in your organization means you must build people up, to communicate with them and share the vision and goals. We've talked about sharing the goal, and later in this book we will talk specifically about communication, but to create the right culture or setting we must build self-esteem within our fellow employees or team members. "Everyone carries around within this invisible backpack full of childhood insecurities," says Captain Michael Abrashoff, from his book, *It's Your Ship*. "Show me a manager who ignores the power of praise, and I'll show you a lousy manager. The same principle applies when you're dealing with your boss. Never tear them down; help them grow strong, anticipate what they want before they want. Make them look good so you will be indispensable."[6] This all has to do with the corporate culture.

In 2006, my commander and good friend, Colonel Chet Roshetko, and I put together a service excellence team in our medical facility at Hurlburt Field, part of Eglin Air Force Base, in Florida. We called ourselves the G-12 (or group of 12). This team was comprised of various positions, ranks, titles, and skillsets, a true mix of our entire hospital. The purpose of this service excellence team (SET) was to create a culture of excellence. We knew that if we created the best possible place to work, this would in turn provide the best customer and patient care. Basically, if you're happy with your employer and satisfied in the work you're doing, you're going to be more productive and take better care of the customer (or in our case, the patient).

There were several initiatives and ideas that we came up with and put into practice. Our mission was to create a setting, or culture, focused on developing and strengthening staff satisfaction. We wanted to help people achieve their personal and professional goals. Within the SET, there were several sub-teams created which oversaw the vision (goals). We called these goals "bricks", as they were the foundation of the SET and our overall vision of success. We rounded on patients and staff, used the 5 fundamentals of communication (known as AIDET®), developed a more robust recognition program, and created a beautiful wall of fame to showcase our high performers. These initiatives collectively are known as the Hurlburt Story, which was our legacy for others to see and follow. Several of those ideas soon became cornerstones in other medical treatment facilities throughout the Air Force.

Steve Gruenert and Todd Whitaker once stated, "The culture of any organization is shaped by the worst behavior the leader is willing to tolerate." What does that mean?

I'll put it in medical terms, because my healthcare background is clinical laboratory. Specimens collected from patients are sent from the emergency department or other areas of the hospital. The laboratory scientist cultures these specimens (grows the bacteria). To create the perfect bacterial culture, there has to be the perfect environment. Each bacterium is nourished by a certain ager or nutritional source for the petri dish. The environment (setting) must be exactly the right temperature, which is 37°C (98°Fahrenheit, or body temp). It must be housed with the right amount of moisture, otherwise the culture will dry out. In addition, for certain cultures, there has to be complete oxygen, and for others a complete lack of oxygen. To have what is considered a pure isolate culture (pure bacteria), these conditions have to be perfect. Any slight variation in any one of these conditions would create an impure culture or allow other bacteria to creep in and choke out the pure culture. What does this mean for the patient? If the laboratory cannot grow the right culture, the doctor cannot diagnose and treat the patient.

This is what happens in many organizations. The inconsistency between departments or within organizations allow other elements to creep in and inhibit the growth of a healthy, strong environment. A culture of accountability exists when an organization consistently performs certain behaviors, using the right tools and techniques, to create the excellence needed to continuously provide the very best product, care, or service at the lowest possible cost. This is high reliability.

Following are several things you can do to create the right setting in your organization. You may not be ready to implement each of them, but they can be stepping stones to bigger ideas and a better place to work.

Welcome New Team Members

At the medical group on Hurlburt Field, we came to understand that if we wanted to make our organization the best in the Air Force, we had to start from the beginning. For us, that beginning was orientation, which we called Medical Group University (or Med Group U). It was designed to be educational and welcoming, so that newcomers would be excited at the prospect of working with us.

When I first arrived at this facility in 2004, I sat through a four-hour, boring session designed to tell me all the things I needed to know but really didn't care about. This may have been the situation when you arrived at your new job, too. This orientation was required by our policies or a governing agency, but it lacked any kind of passion that showed this was a great place to work. It marked the task off the checklist but left much to be desired.

For Med Group U, we revamped this process and made it eight hours, which probably does not sound like an improvement. But, we incorporated fun and games, breakfast and lunch, and a tour of the facility and the military base. We brought in experienced, entertaining speakers to deliver the same information from the old orientation, only presented in a better format. And, we told stories. Again, stories build legends, and legends build legacy. The legacy of the organization, the culture of an organization, is built upon the stories that are told.

We let people know from the beginning that we were excited that they were a part of our organization. The commander (CEO) was present at every orientation to ensure he was highly visible and welcoming. The newcomers were told about available opportunities. We passionately discussed the mission and vision of our organization which got them excited from the start. We had a 97% "exceptional" rating on our orientation surveys, with most people telling us this was the best training they had ever attended.

Imagine, military members who had been a part of as many as a dozen organizations previously, rated us the best.

We also asked our newcomers to complete a dream sheet. This form identified the personal and professional goals of that new employee. Then, that employee's supervisor discussed the information and planned a course of action to help that member attain those goals during their time at that duty location. To keep this in perspective, military members many times were only assigned to an organization for 3-5 years. So, the leaders had just that amount of time to help the newcomer achieve their goals.

People were informed about the difference in the culture, and the setting, of this organization. We told them what they could expect. And if at any time these expectations were not met, they were to let us know. We wanted to correct any variance in that culture. Then, three to five months later, we would bring them back for a three-hour session we called Medical Group University 2 (or U2). At this point, we received feedback about the culture to ensure that the things that we described earlier were taking place. This is called validation. We re-emphasized how valued they were in the organization, engaged them in opportunities, and let them know we had not forgotten about them.

Similarly, at Studer Group we coach organizations to have 30- and 90-day follow-up conversations to talk about what's going well, areas we can improve, and recognition of co-workers of anyone who have helped them employee adapt. And if they're a high-performing employee, we would also ask them if they know anyone else who they thought would be a great fit for this culture. Who better to recruit people to your organization than high-performing people who know other high-performing people? You don't have to pursue what you can attract.

The May 2017 issue of *Harvard Business Review*, has a fantastic article called, "Onboarding Isn't Enough." The author explains that onboarding is an apt term for the way many companies support a leader's transition, because not much more is involved in bringing the executive safely on deck. In fact, according to a global survey of 588 senior executives who had recently transitioned into new roles, organizational culture and politics, not lack of competence or skill, were the primary reasons for failure.[7] Almost 70% of the respondents pointed to a lack of understanding about the norms and practices – poor cultural fit.[8]

In another global survey, 198 human resource executives assessed their organizations onboarding efforts.[9] Most thought their companies did a good job at basic orientation but only half said the organizations were effective in facilitating alignment between leaders and their teams, and fewer than a third said they actually helped executives adapt to the culture.

It is important in our organizations and in our teams that we ensure that everyone has a place, everyone has a purpose, everyone is prepared, and everyone is passionate about what they do. Establish this in the very beginning, when an employee is first hired. At Hurlburt Field, we even contacted people before they left their last duty station, prior to their arrival at our organization, to begin the welcoming process. We welcomed them as part of the team before they even entered the front door. **People want to go where they are celebrated, not merely tolerated.**

Collaboration and Synergy

"If you cannot relate, you cannot connect. If you cannot connect, you cannot collaborate", says the wisest woman I know: my wife, Michelle Noon. I would add, you cannot change, you cannot challenge, and you cannot cooperate without relating.

Collaboration is much more than cooperation. You can cooperate and still not agree. Please do not mistake or interchange the two. Cooperation is what you may see in Congress, but only to avoid catastrophe. There is no synergy. Collaboration involves everybody heading in the same direction together and doing so passionately. We also call this alignment. It is also a coalition. If you're not aligned with the culture of the organization, you will never function well within it.

When you drive east from Destin, Florida, the beach area close to my residence, and you are heading to Panama City Beach, there is only one road to get there, Florida Highway 98. There are two lanes of traffic heading one direction. You don't have to drive in the same lane, you don't have to drive at the same speed, you don't have to drive in the same vehicle, you don't even have to leave at the same time, but you are still going in the same direction to the same goal. Essentially, this is alignment. Some may get to the destination easier or faster. Others may run into delays or may not be as adept as others. Bottom line, alignment is going the same direction.

If you don't have the same goals as the organization and are not in alignment with those that you work with, then it's time to turn off the road and find another place to be. There is nothing wrong with that. Sometimes, it just isn't the right place to be or the right time to be there. You must have the right people on the motor coach, in the right seats, and that bus needs to be going in the right direction.

Teamwork should never just be a slogan. When I coach organizations and they talk about what they do well, I don't let them use the word teamwork. I think it's a catchall that we say to appease those who ask. It's like saying you're great or good when asked how you are, whether you actually are or not. I always dig a little deeper and ask very specifically, "What examples do you have of what teamwork looks like? And even further than that, who exemplifies that teamwork?"

True teams create collaborative efforts for the betterment of the organization. However, simply assigning people to a project does not mean that they have collaboration. To create collaboration in an organization is to effectively get team members "locked in". There must be synergy, or by definition, "mutually advantageous conjunction or compatibility of distinct business participants or elements." **The best corporate cultures are those who intentionally acknowledge peoples' strengths and weaknesses and communicate well to get the job done.** Vince Lombardi once stated, "Individual commitment to a group effort – that is what makes a team work, a company work, a society work, a civilization work."

To create synergy, teams must train together, learn together, motivate together, work together. Imagine if you had a team of volleyball players and each of the positions only trained separately. Hitters trained together; setters trained together; defense trained together. If the team does not spend time together, putting what they know to the test, they will not be able to coordinate on the volleyball floor. Each may do well on their own but putting them together without coordination and collaboration could be disastrous. They would have flawed teamwork. Flawed teamwork is when a group of people assume they are a team, yet each does their own thing.

The same can be said of your business. If the marketing personnel are rebranding the company but the sales team is sending out proposals on old document templates, both teams may have great ideas and efforts, but they are not collaborating to meet the end goal.

There is more than one way to bring collaboration to your team. People are different; they are unique. Depending upon their training, experiences, and knowledge, getting a team to collaborate may take many different methods. Creating respect and a sense of ownership and value between team members will ensure the highest amount of collaborative effort. Putting team members in the right place and in the right position on the team will create that collaboration.

Match People to Projects

In all the different places that I have worked during my 20 years with the Air Force and 6 years with Studer Group®, I've learned something crucial, in regard to people and work. Just because someone is trained to do a job doesn't necessarily make them right for that job. Some people just don't have what it takes, or the job just isn't the right fit for that person. They may not be interested in that job or have the skills to do it. That's ok! You'll find somebody else. This doesn't necessarily mean that because they can't do the job they are of no value to your organization. You just have to find out where the person is most valuable, or they simply may not be the right fit for your organization. We need to get over credentials sometimes. Move beyond the resume. Start looking at people's mentality, personality, character, and values…not just their résumé.

At one point in my military career, I asked my commanding officer if I could be part of the data analysis team. This is a bold move for somebody who was a clinical laboratory director, but I wanted to learn and eventually became the leader of this team. I did fairly well through commitment and hard work, but I soon realized that this was not the right seat for me. I'm even currently in my third role with Studer Group®. I love being part of an organization that wants to match people to the right place, maximizing their potential. It's not that I didn't do well in my first two roles. I just fit better each time I made the move. Now, I am in the job I have dreamed of being in for more than 30 years.

Oprah Winfrey was fired from her first television job because executives thought she was too emotionally involved in her stories. Now she's a billionaire. Right job, wrong place. Lucille Ball was only cast in B movies when she first started her film career. She then found her calling in comedy and became a legend. Film director Ang Lee tried very hard to become an actor, and then he found his calling behind the camera. You never know when you're one move away from your ideal role. Keep growing until you find the right fit.

Reward and Recognition

Reward and recognition has always been an important part of any good organizational culture. I would expand this to include appreciation, because there is a difference. Reward is built upon recognition, but they are not one in the same. Appreciation conveys value, typically when the event occurs, and is sometimes more important to the employee. Yet they are seldom practiced in some organizations. Why is that? I would contend most managers or leaders think they do a great job at recognizing employee performance. Yet time after time, when we ask the employees, the opinions are different.

I once conducted an unofficial poll at an organization where I worked. I asked senior leaders how visible they were in visiting different departments, rounding on sections, and recognizing employees. About 65% said were very visible and available for staff to communicate with. Not a good number, since it should be at 100%. But I then asked staff what their thoughts were about visibility, and the numbers were less than 15%. How is this such a disconnect? Leaders assume they are spending time in connection and relationship, but staff do not view it the same. Why? I determined that perception is reality and leaders do not proactively engage.

Recognition for what we do, especially when we go above and beyond, is a very important part of every person's life. Some people are content with just a pat on the back, others want to be recognized in front of a crowd, given a plaque or trophy, or have their name up in lights. Most appreciate a handwritten note or short e-mail. And still, some people are content with no public recognition at all, just the feeling of satisfaction for a job well done, although there are truly few of them. Sometimes, there are generational differences in how employees prefer to be rewarded and recognized. Other times, by getting to know your employees' dreams and motivators, you'll find special ways to acknowledge their results. And knowing this helps us be better leaders. However you do it, presentation and genuine care are crucial for reward and recognition to have a positive impact.

When I first arrived at Hurlburt Field, quarterly award winners were recognized in a specific spot in a hallway. It was a small framed board with even smaller pictures. To make matters worse, it was located behind a large potted plant, in a corner where no one could see the pictures. To this day, I don't understand how no one saw that as a problem. No one wanted their picture displayed there. It was an unflattering way to recognize winners, so we decided to do something about it. We lined an entire hallway with four 6x4-foot wooden frames with matting and posted all of our award winners and others we wanted to recognize. We began to recognize not just quarterly and yearly award winners; we also put pictures of newcomers on the wall. We recognized people who graduated from different schools, attained Air Force level recognition, or had gotten 100% on their mandated fitness test. We also put up a "brag list." This was where people in the clinic, patients, customers, or staff members, could brag about the great job others had done. The hallway is located in the front of the clinic and every day staff members and patients would walk by and see dozens of people reading about our accomplishments. Just before I transferred to my next duty station, I counted 72 people with their name or picture on those boards. In a hospital that had less than 400 employees, that's incredible participation.

Hand-written notes are another important tool for personal recognition. In 1999 and 2000 while I was in Hawaii, I received two hand-written notes from the base commander, Brigadier General Steve Redmann. To this day, these notes are posted on the bulletin board in my office. His gesture inspired me to do the very same thing for others. I've coached leaders of all levels to send a personalized thank you note to their employees every week by mail to the employee's house, so their families can read about the amazing job they're doing at work. This doesn't take that much time and the benefits to the organization and to the culture are immeasurable.

At one point, one of my teams included two single Airmen, a civilian single mother, and another Airman who was married to someone that worked in our facility. For all four people, I sent thank you notes to their respective families. I remember thanking the children of the single mom, appreciating them at even nine and ten years old. I told him how much their mom meant to the Air Force and told them what a value their mom was to our work. I also recognized how difficult it was that she wasn't always home when they arrived home from school. Those young girls would come to my office when they were visiting their mom at work and spend time with me. I even had a TV in my office and would put on cartoons while they sat with me. This is how leaders connect! By recognizing the commitment of my team, as well as their families, a personal trust was formed.

It's also important to reward team effort. Sometimes, this is harder to do because you can't get everyone together or not everyone contributed to the result. You should ensure that the recognition is appropriate for each team member. How do we do this? Find the best time when most of the team can attend, not just the only time when everyone can. Celebrate multiple times and in different ways, such as alternating shifts, via e-mail or at quarterly trainings. Bring in the highest level of leadership in the organization to ensure recognition is well known.

When you've truly built a culture of recognition, one of the Nine Principles® in the book *Hardwiring Excellence*, this becomes the norm, not an occasional or yearly event. This means we don't just recognize people because it's that time of the month or year. It's not because the leadership needed a nominee for this quarter. It's the rule, not the exception. If I were to walk through your department and ask your highest performing people when the last time was that they were recognized, rewarded, or appreciated for their work, and they say anything less than the past 30 days, I would say you do not have a culture of recognition.

Build a Learning Environment

A culture of recognition and excellence requires an atmosphere where employees feel challenged to learn and grow in their professional and personal lives. The very essence of this book is about fostering a lifelong learner who feels ready and prepared to step in to the next role. These people love a challenge and, more importantly, they love to be challenged. They also love to challenge others. Employees must feel as though their company or team wants to invest in their success. A learning environment creates the challenges and provides resources needed for people to grow. In fact, one of the values of the Studer Group® is intellectual curiosity. We highly encourage people to challenge their learning.

When I was a lab director, I would tell my staff members during feedback sessions that I would stretch them as far as they can be stretched. I would tell them that they could accomplish more than they ever thought possible if they trusted me and let me challenge them. I told them, "At the limit to what you think you can be stretched, I will pull you a little further." And, I told them to let me know if they felt like I was pushing them too hard or challenging them too much. It happened one time. I had a young lab tech who approached me in my office, almost in tears, and said, "You've given me too much." I learned a valuable lesson about high performers and not overloading them.

The Air Force is good at recognizing that the opportunity to learn and grow is essential, but our service excellence team wanted to take it a step further. Since Hurlburt Field is home to Air Force Special Operations (individuals called commandos), we developed Commando Medic University. People in our organization could set up a lunchtime class and teach others any topic they wanted. Sometimes it was about success or financial management; sometimes it was medically related, and other times military issues. We even developed credit hours that could be applied to an Associate, Bachelor's, or Master's "degree," which we would present to the recipients in front of the senior leaders, when each degree was completed. This was a highly successful and motivating opportunity for our staff members.

I've spoken at more than 150 organizations in my time at Studer Group, in sessions we call Leadership Development Institutes. These are one to two day-long leader training sessions held at least quarterly each year. In some organizations we've incorporated Employee Development Institutes, where all employees have the opportunity to learn and grow. The emphasis in this type of learning environment is that employees are valued not just for their job or the work they do, but for who they are.

It is essential to understand that if you don't live by design, you live by default. Status quo is not an option for any highly reliable and high performing organization or team. **A learning environment creates assets with and takes away your liabilities, therefore creating true value.** A learning environment creates problem solvers. Problem solvers are a valuable asset to the team.

I learned from Dr. A. R. Bernard, the pastor of the Christian Cultural Center in New York City, that, "Problem solvers never diminish what is in their hand; there is always something they can use. Every time a person solves a problem they are elevated to the next level, because you cannot solve a problem at the same level in which it was created". Teaching people how to be problem solvers in a culture that allows learning, growing, and developing in their environment will bring value to your employees. In addition to being problem solvers, I've taught many organizations how to be critical thinkers who can identify the problem and solve it. "We live life on levels and we arrive in stages," Dr. Bernard teaches. "Each new level takes a person to new knowledge, authority, and responsibility."

If organizations can sense and respond to emerging opportunities, there is a good chance they will endure and survive any economic situation. If they can perceive and respond to each new opportunity with greater ingenuity and speed—that is, if they can get better at getting better—there is a good chance they will blossom.

What if a group of people at your organization decided to set up a library in the lunchroom? They stocked the library with books on leadership, learning, brand management, and anything else that might help employees contribute more to the organization. Now instead of reading the newspaper during lunch and eating alone, people pick up a book and then talk about what they've read. Can you see it? Managers sitting side by side with people who work in the mailroom and hear them talking about how to improve the company's brand. Or consider hosting a lunchtime speaker on topics like, giving and receiving feedback, investing, or negotiations. While these topics may help people in their jobs, they may also help them buy their next car or save for their children's college tuition. When people talk after work with their family or friends, they are now apt to say, "You know what I learned today?" That's a beautiful conversation.

As long as learning is viewed by employees as the latest fad you're introducing, your culture will not become one of learning. To cement the elements of learning into your organization's culture, you'll need to ensure that new ways of asking questions, running meetings, and conducting performance reviews become your organization's new routine. Leaders who consistently and energetically reinforce the value of learning serve as the reactor core of an organization where people learn.

If leaders want to create adaptive organizations capable of getting better at getting better, they must first look at how people learn in the workplace and develop a plan to create a learning culture. A learning environment encourages individuals to apply what they learned. Application is the evidence of learning. Are you able to apply this to your work, your personal life, your family? Are you and your organization clear about how much you value learning? If you aren't emulating this practice, you won't be able to inspire others to learn. As a leader, you set an example for everyone in the organization. Invest in their success and your own. Own your future or be disrupted by it.

Standards of Behavior

Another element of a growing, thriving culture is the use of, and accountability to, standards of behavior. How else can we have consistency between leadership and departments if we don't have standards by which we call out misbehavior? I don't think we should all be robots who act in exactly the same way, but there has to be a standard by which we measure acceptable performance and behavior. As my pastor, Steve Vaggalis, would say, "Standards either confine you, or they define you."

Think of standards of behavior as a fence around your yard. The fence defines the property line of the family household. There's a certain element in the culture of the Noon family that you will experience when you enter our yard or the front door. You will experience hospitality, because that is the environment my wife has created. There are rules, which seemed confining to my kids at times, but defined their character. The same holds true within your department or organization. When people enter the facility where you work, it won't take long for them to get a sense of your organization's culture. They will define your organization by the setting they experience and, in turn, emulate. Standards of behavior aligns behavior throughout the organization which gives people a sense of the culture.

Some examples of standards of behavior in organizations are:
- Smile when you meet every customer, patient, or client. Escort them to their location.
- Introduce yourself to each person you meet. Acknowledge them with a handshake or smile.
- Give the duration or expected wait time so people are not frustrated or agitated if service gets behind.
- Explain the process or procedure to reduce anxiety and improve the compliance of our client or customer.
- Thank people at every occasion for choosing this business.

This setting puts us in the ready position for growth, change, increase, improvement and, most importantly, leadership.

Does your organization or team have a story? What is that story?

_____

_____

_____

_____

_____

What is the current condition of your setting?

_____

_____

_____

_____

_____

What elements of cultural change are you going to implement this week?
This month?

_____

_____

_____

_____

_____

The Setting

Culture
Create it
Nurture it
Define it — Standard
Talk about it
Right person & Place
Reward & Recognize

Learn

Always bear in mind that your own resolution to success is more important than any other one thing.

– Abraham Lincoln

4

Ready Position:
The Key to A Great Set
Is to Be Prepared

I watched the setter as she prepared to set up the outside hitter. Every time a pass went in the air, she would get to the ready position by the net. She was never caught unprepared. The hitter was in position just to the left of the side line. The middle hitter was five steps back from the net. I learned that day that these are the ready positions. Volleyball is a game of speed; speed wins matches. If everyone is in the right spot, the plays move faster. If everyone is ready, they execute with precision and accuracy.

My wife and I grew up in Michigan's Upper Peninsula on the border of Wisconsin. I had no choice but to be a Green Bay Packers fan then, but I am still a strong and willing participant. We grew up hearing stories about Vince Lombardi, the legendary coach who led the Packers to victory in the first two Super Bowls. My wife's grandparents owned a supper club in Green Bay and were often treated to tales from Packers players and coaches that frequented the restaurant. Vince was the epitome of a coach. I think I've heard and read every quote he ever said or was made about him. Things like, "When Coach Lombardi told you to sit down, you didn't look for a chair." Or, "Winning isn't a sometime thing, it's an all the time thing." My favorite quote was, **"Perfect practice makes perfect."**

Over the years, I've heard many people say practice makes perfect, but I think Vince Lombardi had it right. I live by the perfect practice makes perfect motto, which is reflected in my home life and in my work. My wife and I have instilled this message in our children as well. We've taught them that preparation precedes position. If they practice poorly they will play poorly. Similarly, if you manage poorly when you're a new manager and don't grow, you will continue to manage poorly if you become a senior manager. Your private practice will determine your public performance. Positive outcomes are achieved by practicing and being prepared. What we prepare for reveals what we value.

Samuel Johnson, the great English author, said, "What we hope ever to do with ease, we must learn first to do with diligence." In layman's terms, boxing champions are not made in the ring, they are only recognized there. The years of preparation that go into becoming an elite athlete or an influential leader are many times never known to the public. People don't walk into a company and immediately become a senior vice president. They put in the work and practice. They learn the business. They learn the game. The best and the brightest have become the best and the brightest because they have chosen to learn and to grow, to yearn and to know more than anyone else.

The pianist, Arthur Rubenstein said, "If I don't practice for a day, I notice. If I don't practice for two days, the orchestra notices. If I don't practice for three days, the world notices." Ted Williams, baseball superstar of the 1940s and 50s, was known as a natural hitter. Once, he was asked about this ability and replied, "There is no such thing as a natural born hitter. I became a good hitter because I paid the price of constant practice."

Practice is perfected with validation, having others study your methods and pay particular attention to your work. The late Jim Rohn, mentor to the likes of Tony Robbins and Mark Victor, once said, "We must all suffer from one of two pains: the pain of discipline or the pain of regret. The difference is discipline weighs ounces while regret weighs tons." Validation is the proof, the authentication of what we have practiced. What good does it do to teach a skill, have others practice it, and then not validate that the teaching is actually working, behaviors have changed, or the student gets better?

I practice every week to perfect my craft of public speaking. I want to be an intentional communicator. Speaking is a performance art; I want to be a master artist. To do that, I study the art of body language: where I should position myself on stage when presenting, what gestures elicit responses from the audience, who to communicate the message most effectively. I exercise my voice to perfect my tone and elevation in pitch.

Just as we discussed getting direction for yourself first before providing direction to others, you must first be prepared in order to help prepare others.

Be Gritty

In the book *Grit: The Power of Passion and Perseverance* by Angela Duckworth, Angela's study of the best of the National Spelling Bee unearths some interesting realities. "Who took home the trophy? A thirteen-year-old named Kerry Close. It was her fifth consecutive year of competition. I estimated she had accumulated at least 3,000 hours of practice." Unsurprisingly, she found that grittier spellers practiced more than their less gritty competitors. But, her most important finding was that the type of practice mattered tremendously. Deliberate practice predicted advancement to further rounds in final competition far better than any other kind of preparation. She continues, "If you judge practice by how much it improves your skill, then deliberate practice has no rival. If, however, we judge practice by what it *feels* like, you might come to a different conclusion. On average, spellers rated deliberate practice as significantly more *effortful*, and significantly less *enjoyable*." So, if we want to be the best leader, employee, or person, deliberate actions lead to definitive results.

Being ready to step in is about being set up for success. The definition of step is, "to take a particular course of action…and each stage is a gradual process." You cannot get from one level to another without taking a step. Each step was set up by your deliberate preparation. Each person you set up can then step in to the next level.

Know Your Strengths and Weaknesses

I truly believe that if a person concentrates on their strengths, their weaknesses will take care of themselves. Business coach, Dan Sullivan says, "If you spend too much time working on your weaknesses, all you end up with is a lot of strong weaknesses." You have to know what your strengths are, as well as your weaknesses.

Sometimes, your greatest strength can also be your greatest weakness. Greatness rests not in being strong, but in the correct use of strength. If you want to change the effect, you have to change the cause. My son is quite athletic and extremely energetic; he always has been. That energy and strength has always been a great asset to him on a football field. However, that energy also made it very difficult for him to concentrate in the classroom. He has had to learn how to harness that energy. Knowing his strengths and his weaknesses makes him a better student and a better athlete.

Knowing your weaknesses and communicating them to others can allow them to use their strengths to help stabilize your weaknesses. Similarly, you have the ability to use your strengths to lift up others. That is the whole idea of the team. Knowing yourself, knowing that you can't do it all by yourself, allows others to be involved in your life. It allows others to help you to become the better manager or the better coach or the better player. It helps you to become a better employee, friend, or spouse. Focus on your strengths and let others help you with your weakness. Look for those mentors, leaders, managers, or friends who can help you become the best you can be.

To leverage your strengths and improve upon your weaknesses, you first need to identify them. Below, list the attributes that best describe your strengths and weaknesses in order, with the first being what represents you the most. Don't list what you think you want to be, list what you are.

Strengths	Weaknesses
_____	_____
_____	_____
_____	_____
_____	_____
_____	_____

Learn

Now that you've identified what your strengths are, it's important to learn everything you can about what it is you want to be prepared for. Early on in my Air Force career, I knew what my goals were and I knew what I wanted to accomplish. I wanted to be the best leader I could be. I watched leaders and managers over the years – some good, some not so good – to understand different leadership styles and tactics. I knew that to accomplish my goals, I had to finish my education and get my commission in the Air

Force. In my free time, I read books about leadership. I wasn't in a leadership position yet, but I knew where I wanted to go and what I wanted to do. I prepared. I'm still preparing. I don't want to ever settle for less than my very best. If you want to change your outcome, you have to change the investment. You invest in what you value.

I joined the Air Force late in life, compared to the traditional military path. I was 26 and I had no formal education prior to enlisting. I didn't finish my bachelor's degree until I was 34. I completed my master's degree at 38. Through the course of my education, I worked part-time in addition to my full-time Air Force duties. I also balanced my time so I could coach soccer for my kids. Of course, all of this could not have been done without the tremendous support of my wife, Michelle. She wanted these things as much as I did. We sacrificed a lot of time to continue to grow. Learning always, growing always. That's how you get there. And it's best to get there together.

When an airman first enters their career in the Air Force, they're sent to a technical school to learn their trade. At their first assignment (duty station), their only job is to learn that trade. Many times, they aren't allowed to further their college education until they have first mastered their primary job. It should be no different in our learning and preparation – one step at a time. When I coach leaders in organizations, they are always impatient to get results. It's understandable, as this is what I was hired to help them do. But, we cannot get to step G without first going through A, B, C, D, E, and F. Sequence and pace is the proper management of change and progress.

When I aspired to be promoted, which in turn would make for a higher paycheck, I was inspired by something I heard Dr. A. R. Bernard say, "You don't get paid for your time, you get paid for your value. If you want to get paid more, become more valuable." How do you become more valuable? Learn. The above average CEO in America reads 60+ books per year. Why? To learn. Remember, preparation comes before promotion.

I am sure there are many of you who aspire to do things above or beyond what you are currently doing. Yet, while you're preparing to become or do whatever your goal is, you must continue to do well in your current position. You can still prepare for the future and take good care of the present. It is a matter of integrity and excellence to continue to do your best while trying to become better.

Sacrifice

A mentor once told me, **"Sometimes you have to go through it, to get to it."** Or, another way I have heard it said, "Sometimes you have to go through what you're going through, to get through what you're going through." You have to pay the price.

As my kids have grown up playing sports, my wife and I have pushed them to be the best they could be. No, we're not the overbearing parents that sacrifice everything to make sure our kids are the best. We knew a parent who scheduled her daughter for an average of 3-4 hours of workouts each day, in addition to her normal school activities. We knew that was too much for our kids and our family, but we worked with our kids. We asked them what they wanted to accomplish in their sport.

Once our children established their goals, we committed to some sacrifice of our own, if they sacrificed what they could to achieve those goals. We told them, "If you want to be the best, you need to make it happen and we will help you any way we can." We took our kids to some of the best trainers in their sports, found some of the best coaches, and bought books and materials that would help them become the best they could be, not necessarily the best of all.

A typical routine for my kids included stretching four times a week, ankle exercises three times a week, and jump rope two times a week. They would run, lift weights, and then practice their individual skills. We did not make them do any of this; this work was their self-discipline in action. We discussed with them the practice and the sacrifice they had to make to accomplish their goals, but they were the ones who ultimately made it happen.

I remember my son's first week of college when he started working out with the football team. He texted me one day and said that he didn't like playing college football. I was a little worried, so I called him. Nothing bad had happened, except that he had gone through one of the most strenuous workouts he had ever endured. He now knew what it took to be a college football player and wasn't sure if he was willing to make that sacrifice, but after reflecting upon his long-term goals and the price required, he decided to stick with it. His scholarship provided the opportunity to play four years of college football and allowed him to graduate with very little student loan debt. Commitment is the price you pay to grow.

Remember what I said before; if you don't live by design you live by default. To design, plan, and practice will bring great results. However, to just allow life to happen by default will bring you nowhere. Sometimes, you have to go through what you're going through, to get through what you're going through. Obstacles won't keep us from victory; it is our view of the obstacles that will keep us from that victory. Maximum impact can never be a result of marginal input. Again, you invest in that which you value. Good enough is the enemy of excellence.

I've heard it said that above average jobs, with above average pay, only go to people with above average ability. Ability comes through sacrifice, practice, and true preparation. Not every athlete has tremendous talent, many just have above average desire. Stability and consistency will increase the ability by practicing over, and over, and over again.

In "The Making of an Expert", *Harvard Business Review* illustrates the grit that it takes to get to the top. "Back in 1985, Benjamin Bloom, a professor of education at the University of Chicago, published a landmark book, *Developing Talent in Young People*, which examined the critical factors that contribute to talent. He took a deep retrospective look at the childhoods of 120 elite performers who had won international competitions or awards in fields ranging from music and the arts to mathematics and neurology. Surprisingly, Bloom's work found no early indicators that could have predicted the virtuosos' success. Subsequent research indicating that there is no correlation between IQ and expert performance in fields such as chess, music, sports, and medicine has borne out his findings. The only innate differences that turn out to be significant—and they matter primarily in sports—are height and body size."[1]

"So, what does correlate with success? One thing emerges very clearly from Bloom's work: all the superb performers he investigated had practiced intensively, had studied with devoted teachers, and had been supported enthusiastically by their families throughout their developing years. Later research building on Bloom's pioneering study revealed that the amount and quality of practice were key factors in the level of expertise people achieved. Consistently and overwhelmingly, the evidence showed that experts are always made, not born. These conclusions are based on rigorous research that looked at exceptional performance using scientific methods that are verifiable and reproducible."[2]

It continues, "The journey to truly superior performance is neither for the faint of heart nor for the impatient. The development of genuine expertise requires struggle, sacrifice, and honest, often painful self-assessment. There are no shortcuts. It will take you at least a decade to achieve expertise, and you will need to invest that time wisely, by engaging in "deliberate" practice— practice that focuses on tasks beyond your current level of competence and comfort. You will need a well-informed coach (like those at Studer Group) not only to guide you through deliberate practice but also to help you learn how to coach yourself. Above all, if you want to achieve top performance as a manager and a leader, you've got to forget the folklore about genius that makes many people think they cannot take a scientific approach to developing expertise."[3]

One of the most remarkable things about preparing for success is that preparation itself will attract opportunities to you. Earl Nightingale is quoted as saying, "If a person does not prepare for his success, when the opportunity comes, it will only make him look foolish." It may be that you are in the gym shooting baskets at all hours of the day, and, unknown to you, were being watched by a college coach. You may think you are the only one on the volleyball court continually hitting balls, setting balls, preparing for your future and someone noticed you. You're diligently working the evening or overnight shift, maybe as the only person in the department. You do everything well and you may think no one notices, but your preparation and diligence will pay off. Someone will recognize your work. Don't quit.

President Dwight D. Eisenhower said, "In preparing…plans are useless, but planning is indispensable." When things change, your response to that change will have a good outcome because you planned. Planning takes sacrifice. Planning takes time. When you plan for different scenarios, that preparation pays big dividends in your ability to adapt and overcome. Preparing for success involves setting aside time yourself: time to train, time to learn, and time to listen. In doing so, you will become more confident and prepared. Successful people plan their day and look back in the evening and see what they've accomplished. For me, it's about creating lists. I love to list all my tasks for each day then check them off to see what I have accomplished. Everything you do is either moving you toward your goal or away from it. Everything you do is either helping or hurting you. Self-sacrifice, self-denial – these practices are not for the faint of heart. You will never get it done if you are always waiting to start until tomorrow.

Even the most menial of practices can make a monumental difference in your performance. John Wooden, the famed basketball coach at UCLA, preached careful preparation. On the first day of his basketball camps, he would sit on the gym floor in front of all these young athletes and take off his basketball shoes and socks. He would then put a new pair of white socks on each foot. He would show the players how to avoid blisters by meticulously smoothing out the wrinkles in their socks. He said, "Even the smallest, most routine preparation counts. Do the right thing over and over every day."

Have you ever heard stories about lottery winners? So often, they win millions of dollars but are totally unprepared to handle that much money. Similarly, you see star athletes going into the NBA or the NFL that are fully prepared to execute the job they have trained to do, but unprepared to handle success and celebrity. Whatever it is you think you want, you need to be prepared for it. Whatever your vision for success, while you are working or on achieving it, you must grow yourself into the kind of person you need to be to manage that success. There is no secret to success. It is simple preparation. As Abraham Lincoln said, "I will study and prepare myself, and someday my chance will come." When there is no sacrifice, that which we attain means so much less.

Groundwork

Inability has more to do with attitude than ability. Responsibility is simply a response to your ability. Ability creates demand and the right of expectation, which demands a greater level of performance. As ability increases through preparation, so does the power of attraction. **The more you are prepared and the more you increase your abilities, the more people will be attracted to you who you can then set up for success and may set you up for success in turn.** What and who we attract in life is determined by the type of person we've chosen to be. I learned a long time ago, in reading books by John Maxwell and others, that you can never attract others to you unless you've attained a higher level of ability. If your level of leadership or talent is at a seven, you'll never attract an eight or nine. Therefore, you have to increase your abilities and talent to increase your leadership capability, before you have the opportunity to lead others. Henry Wadsworth Longfellow once wrote, "The heights a great man reached and kept were not attained by sudden flight. But they, while their companions slept, were toiling upward in the night." You have to lay the groundwork.

One of my favorite family movies of the 90s was *Iron Will*. In it, a young boy, Will Stoneman, takes on a man-sized task of a long dogsled race to win $10,000 to save his family's farm. Will was trained by a Native American friend. On the first morning of his training, he is awoken and dragged outside in only his long john underwear. Throughout his training, Will is taught how to endure cold and harsh conditions and eat very little food, to lighten his load for the dogs. He gets less and less sleep each night to prepare to work longer and harder than the other competitors. By doing so, he not only wins the race but the hearts of Americans.

I met one of my best military friends during my Air Force training. His name was Mike. We were both lab technicians and later were fortunate to be stationed together in central Georgia. We also worked part-time delivering pizza for a few months that first summer. Everything was a competition for us, from our work in the Air Force to how fast we could deliver a pizza. He was rather inquisitive, and always wanted to be prepared for everything. He was also quite adventurous.

During the night shift, Mike would take apart some of the machines that we used. He wanted to see how they worked so that if there was ever a problem he knew how to fix it. He was always reading and studying, preparing for his certification and his future. Mike truly embodied preparation before promotion. He was always prepared. He laid the groundwork for his future.

Unfortunately, that future didn't happen. Mike passed away in 1993, while living that adventurous life on a hiking trail in North Georgia. Three days later, I escorted Mike's body home for his final rest. I met his family, shared stories, and had the great privilege and honor to present his mom with the United States flag that covered his casket and was folded by the Air Force honor guard. It was the most difficult, and yet most honorable, thing I have ever done. For the last 25+ years, Mike's picture has traveled with me and continuously graces my desk. Every day, when I sit there, I'm reminded to be prepared. To live life to its fullest. To lay the groundwork. To appreciate the sacrifice. I hope you do too.

Entered Into Eternal Rest
Sunday, Nov. 14, 1993

So now we've come to a point where you understand the responsibility of being a setter, a leader, a mentor, or a coach. You've gotten direction. You understand the role and responsibility of setting yourself up for success. You've created the setting. You are prepared. Now you can begin the process of setting others up for success. Remember application is the evidence of learning. You've applied it to yourself now it's time to apply it to others.

What things will you learn, practice, or sacrifice to ensure you make it to your goal?

_____
_____
_____
_____
_____

What things will you stop doing to keep yourself on the learning, self-sacrificing path?

_____
_____
_____
_____
_____

It is not the critic who counts, not the man who points out how the strong man stumbled, or where the doer of deeds could have done better. The credit belongs to the man who is actually in the arena, whose face is marred by dust and sweat and blood, who strives valiantly, who errs and comes short again and again, who knows the great enthusiasms, the great devotions, and spends himself in a worthy cause, who at best knows achievement and who at worst if he fails at least fails while daring greatly so that his place shall never be with those cold and timid souls who know neither victory nor defeat.

– Theodore Roosevelt

5

Jump Set – Jump Serve:
Motivating Your Team

As I watched the game, I noticed the tempo kept getting faster. Everyone knew their place; everyone knew their responsibility. Instead of walking up to the line and hitting the ball over the net, the server would run, throw the ball up in the air, jump, and hit the ball over the net. Her jump-serve seemed to motivate the team. I noticed as the pace of the game intensified, the setter, instead of just approaching the net to place the ball, would jump and then set the ball. Every time there was a jump-serve or a jump-set, the team's motivation and enthusiasm increased. The other team couldn't keep up. I was told, "Speed wins games." The team's collective speed and intensity created momentum and helped motivate them to another win.

It is the responsibility of every leader and every coach to motivate the team. A lack of motivation decreases productivity by billions of dollars and can cause employees to become disengaged in their work.[1] Motivation is essential to job satisfaction and, more importantly, engagement. First, you must learn how to motivate yourself before you can motivate others, just as we have to prepare and set ourselves up for success before we can help others. Just as a doctor prescribes a medication to get a response, not a reaction, a leader should be skilled to prompt a response from their team.

There are intrinsic and extrinsic motivators which lead to high performance. Intrinsic motivation occurs when people proactively engage in certain activities or hobbies for the personal reward. The athlete who has the inner strength and desire to be the best is motivated by that desire. Extrinsic motivation comes from the outside, from some other person or situation, to earn a reward or avoid punishment. A cheering crowd may motivate an athlete to perform at a higher level.

There are no magic formulas for motivating employees. Much of the effectiveness of motivation in your organization will rely on leaders and distinguished members. Like any other skill or art, consistent practice will make perfect execution. The more one polishes their motivational skills, the better and more capable she or he becomes. Leaders have the responsibility of fostering growth in the next generation but, without a strategically planned process, motivation will never work.

Motivation, to paraphrase General Dwight Eisenhower, is about getting other people to do something because they want to do it. As a leader, you must create a desirable, productive work environment where employees can find challenges and be rewarded. Motivation is not nice to have, it is absolute; you must have it!

By definition, motivation is the set of reasons that determines one to engage in a particular behavior.[2] According to various theories, motivation may be rooted in the basic need to minimize physical pain and maximize pleasure, or it may include specific needs, a desired object goal, or an ideal state.[3] There are several different theories about motivation, such as the need-achievement theory, interest theory, goal-setting theory, or self-determination theory. While I will not go into the details of those theories, I would encourage you to investigate them and consider their applications.

The jump-set or jump-serve in a game of volleyball creates many advantages. It improves the speed of the game and provides opportunities to score points. Increasing your advantage in a game, or in a business, is a motivator itself. In the same manner, using the tools of motivation, you can create many advantages for your staff and team.

The number one way to motivate people is to build them up, instilling in them a pride in their organization, their team, and themselves. Employees need to know that they're valued. They need to know you trust them, have confidence in their abilities, that you care about them and their families, and they need to hear it often. Their success needs to be recognized and rewarded. Their shortcomings need to be coached, to know that you will invest in their success.

As I described in chapter two, there are four behavioral characteristics of great leadership. The four outcomes of those practices are simply this: value, trust, care, and communication.

Value What They Value

"What you value is an expression of your character," says Dr. A. R. Bernard. "And character determines your destiny. If you cease to value something, you will eventually lose it."

Students at a junior high school in Chicago were studying the Seven Wonders of the World. At the end of the lesson, the students were asked to list what they considered to be the new Seven Wonders of the World. The following received the most votes:
1. The Great Pyramids of Giza
2. The Taj Mahal in India
3. The Grand Canyon in Arizona
4. The Panama Canal
5. The Empire State Building
6. St. Peter's Basilica
7. The Great Wall of China

While gathering the votes, the teacher noted that one student, a quiet girl, hadn't yet turned in her paper. She asked the girl if she was having trouble with her list. The quiet girl replied, "Yes, a little. I couldn't quite make up my mind because there were so many." The teacher said, "Well, tell us what you have, and maybe we can help." The girl hesitated, then read, "I think the Seven Wonders of the World are:
1. To touch
2. To taste
3. To see
4. To hear
5. To feel
6. To laugh
7. To love."[4]

It is amazing how this little girl in middle school knew what was most valuable in life, and yet sometimes we lose sight of that over time.

As a leader or coach, you must instill or infuse value into the people on your team. Value is created when we show interest and concern for their well-being. Value is produced when we take interest in their family. Value is fashioned when we take interest in what interests them. We give others value when we let them know their ideas are important. They gain value by knowing their work is important. I've heard it said that if you want to know what someone values, take a look at their checkbook or, in this day and age, their credit card statements. What we invest in financially shows what we value. It's funny to watch people who will spend lavishly on things they enjoy but will drive three extra miles to save four cents on a gallon of gas. It's what that individual values.

Going a step further, what we invest our time in also shows what we value. The people I work with know I respect and value time. They know I will be on time to meetings and when completing projects because I firmly believe that being on time shows that I value others' time. In fact, I often quote Vince Lombardi's philosophy, "Ten minutes early is on time, on time is late, and late means you'd better not show up."

When it comes to people, Dale Carnegie gives some of the best advice I have ever heard. In his book *How to Win Friends and Influence People*, Carnegie wisely said, "You can make more friends in two months by becoming interested in other people than you can in two years by trying to get other people interested in you."[5] I think he was referring to valuing other people. "Remember that a person's name is to that person the sweetest and most important sound in any language," he said. "If you want to win friends, make it a point to remember them. If you remember my name, you pay me a subtle compliment; you indicate that I have made an impression on you. Remember my name to add to my feeling of importance."[6] We instill value and add to their feelings of being important to others by making this personal connection.

This is important in most situations. It became very evident to me during my time in the military, where members are addressed by their rank. When a commander would ask me to do something and she or he said, "Sergeant Noon (or in later years, Major Noon), will you…," I always responded, "Yes, Ma'am" or "Yes, Sir," as was my duty. But when they said, "Mark, would you do…," I was much more likely to do it quicker, with a greater feeling of responsibly and worth. If they chose to use my first name I would respond more enthusiastically, with a feeling of greater importance and value. I value when people use my name.

I do the very same thing today. When I speak to a group, I always look to connect to people by using their name. Many times, if the group is 50 or less, I can remember most everyone's name, and use them in my stories or in my visualizations while speaking. The people in the audience will come to me after, commenting on how many names I remembered and ask me how I do it. It is not a special gift or skill I have; it's just something that is important to me, so I work very hard at it. There is no sweeter sound in any language than the sound of one's own name, and because I value it I want to instill that same value in others. It's what I refer to as the "value connection." In the wise words of Aretha Franklin, "R.E.S.P.E.C.T, find out what it means to me."

We inculcate value in our organization and with our team by valuing what they value. By adding value to those around you, you're investing in women and men with the potential of exponentially multiplying your influence. Find out what it is they value. I have a very good friend who values time off over all other forms of reward or recognition. She loves vacation time, so giving her a day off as a reward is a huge win for her. Some employees value a monetary bonus, while some like to be recognized with an award or through public acknowledgement.

Take the extra step to find out what your teammates each value when being recognized and reward them with it. Find out what they value in their job or their place on the team and put them in that position or give them that responsibility. Instill value, be concerned with your people's personal values, and invest in their success and personal lives.

Value is essentially what you think is most important. If you have children, they are likely what you value most. Even when your baby reaches into his diaper after a nap and smears *what was in his diaper* all over the wall, you still value him. Even when your toddler loudly exclaims in a department store, "Daddy, your butt is too big," you still value and cherish every moment with her, though it may cause you to walk out of the store with a new pair of (more flattering) pants.

Communicate Your Appreciation

It's crucial to organizational success that you communicate to individuals how important they are to the team and organization. Sometimes it's as simple as a pat on the shoulder or a thank you note for doing a great job. Remember how we discussed thank you notes in chapter three?

One of my technicians at the Special Operations Base at Hurlburt Field was from Atlanta. I sent a note to his mom, since I knew how much he appreciated and loved her, to let her know that her son had just won the quarterly award for the best non-commissioned officer in our hospital. I told her what a valuable asset her son was to our organization, how proud we were to have him on our team, and how proud she should be of her son. I thanked her for raising such a fine young man. His mom called me the day she got her thank you note to let me know how much that meant to her. For her son, it showed how much I valued him. For the next year, whenever he would get calls from his mom during the duty day she would always ask to speak with me. Sometimes our conversations would carry on longer than the ones she would have with her son.

When individuals feel appreciated, it increases their motivation to do a good job. Thank you notes are a great way to do this, but they are not the only way. Organizations often use surveys to receive feedback about how employees feel about their work experience. A typical question I've seen on surveys is, "What are some ideas for making this place better?" Often, the employee offers an idea for improvement and wonders if someone will actually listen. Invariably, people give great ideas, yet they seldom receive any follow-up.

Once, while I was teaching a leadership development session at an organization in the central valley of California, the CEO shared the results of their recent employee survey. They were sure to communicate to the team that, through the survey, they collected 1,600 ideas for organizational improvement. Wow! The CEO was excited to begin acting upon the ideas and was quick to provide plans for their review and implementation.

Like this CEO, you must listen to what your individual employees are saying and act on their input. As leaders, you need to show them that you value their feedback to make your organization a great place to work. You may not act on every idea you receive, but it is critical that you communicate that the ideas submitted are heard and valued. This means that organization must address all 1,600 ideas. The submitter should be notified whether their idea was doable or not, with a timeframe for implementation or an explanation for why it would not be implemented.

You also show you care by being concerned. Good leaders are concerned about their employees' families, their careers, their education, and their own personal values or beliefs. In every organization that I have led or been a part of, my number one concern has always been the concerns of my fellow employees. This practice should be instilled within every person on the team which will, in turn, influence the entire organization. When one person has a family concern that needs to be addressed, the rest of the team is invested in their wellbeing. That means we sacrifice for one another by covering their shift or section, taking a shorter lunch, or staying late at work. We bring value to other people, teammates, and fellow employees by caring about their concerns.

In healthcare organizations, I teach providers to ask patients right away what concerns them most about their visit. Many times, it's not just what's in the medical record. By addressing concerns early on, they save time and build a better connection with the patient.

Build Trust by Investing in Their Success

The word invest means to commit something, such as money or time, in order to gain a return; to devote oneself to a purpose; to endow with authority or power; to surround with troops or ships.[7] That means when we invest in other people's lives we are committing ourselves to them, showing them that they are valued. The things people invest in show what they value. Remember how I said earlier to take a look at a person's check book or their credit card statement to see what is of value to them? Investing in others is a sure-fire way to motivate them and to instill trust. This action says that you are banking on a person and their outcomes to drive your own success and that you believe they will succeed. I find it interesting that, in the definition of invest, the dictionary talks about surrounding with troops and giving authority and power. When we support the people we work with, surrounding them and protecting them, we give them the power and the authority to do their job or their task to the very best of their ability.

Having served in the military for as long as I did, I have a great respect for the protection that the military has provided the people of the United States. And, because I know that I'm surrounded and protected as a citizen, I then have the power and the ability to do the things that I want to do, and the freedom with which to do them. The Bill of Rights enables me to do so and the troops defend and protect that constitutional right.

Investing in the lives of others requires commitment. The day that I married my wife Michelle, I told her, "I do." With that statement, I committed myself to investing in her life until I die. In turn, my wife and I invest in the success of our children. We invested money and time in preparing our kids for the activities they wanted to participate in. We committed ourselves to ensuring their spiritual health. We committed our time to helping with homework, so they could get good grades to be able to attend the college of their choice. It takes commitment to invest in others.

When I give authority or power to people that I work with, allowing them to make decisions in my stead, I am committed to supporting those decisions. I will never shirk my responsibility for my workplace. Those who work with me know that I will back them up and take responsibility for shared mistakes. The team gets credit for the wins, but the coach takes responsibility for the losses. It is important that in decision-making there is no retribution for making bad decisions. There are consequences to the things that we do, but we can't condemn people for deciding. To invest in people is to teach them how to make good decisions.

When my daughter, Bailey, was 13 years old, she was torn between playing volleyball and soccer. We coached her through that decision-making process. We didn't want to influence her decision to play one sport or the other. We gave her the authority to make that decision, with the understanding that we would support whatever she chose. We protected her with advice and surrounded her with support. Over the years, we had invested enough time and effort into teaching her how to make good decisions. Therefore, we knew that even at 13 she could make a good decision. She decided on playing volleyball and, as of this writing, she is finishing her senior year playing at a Division 1 college.

Another way to invest in the success of the people you work with is to look for educational opportunities. As a director, I sought opportunities for my staff to grow their skills within their talents or interests. Those could be internal, within the organization, or external, which would require time, travel, or some monetary investment to attend. Over the years, I have observed many managers who will create opportunities for themselves and not for the people that work for them. If the coach on the team is the only one learning the game, how does it benefit the team? If the coach is learning so they can continue to invest in the team, then great, but there must be a balance of opportunities. Every leader needs to check their motives.

When it comes to motivating people, there is no one style, theory, or way to make it happen. Maslow's hierarchy of needs says we must meet basic needs before we can meet their motivating needs. Whether you are using Alderfer's ERG theory of hierarchical needs, McClellan's acquired needs theory – or any other theory, for that matter – as the leader, manager, or setter, it is your responsibility to encourage and motivate those around you. Psychologists tell us, and every personality test out there shows us, that there are four types of personalities. Some are very dominant or controlling, while others are outgoing and amiable. Others are very dependable and good listeners. And yet others are highly conscientious, detailed people, who take pride in a job well done. Before investing in a person's development it's crucial to know what kind of person they are in order to have the most impact. Know your people and what motivates them.

I have a friend that I run with on the weekends. He is 15 years my junior, so his pace is a little faster. When we run, he slows his pace down a bit to match my speed. After 6-7 miles of this, I fade off and he continues on at a bit faster pace, for another 3-4 miles. During one of our recent runs we had to cross a bridge. The bridge was narrow and required us to run single file, rather than side-by-side as we did on the road. My friend likes to run in the front because he says it motivates him more, knowing someone is fast on his heels, so I let him take the lead. I like to be on the heels of the person in front, so I can keep pace and blow by them at the end. This is how I am motivated. We train well together, knowing each other's strengths, weaknesses, and motivators.

Instill Pride

A great way to build trust is to instill pride in your staff for the work they do. As I mentioned, when new hires first arrived at the hospital at Hurlburt Field, they were put through Medical Group University. From the onset, they were instilled with pride in the opportunity that lay before them. They were told about the exciting things the organization had accomplished and the wonderful people that worked there. They were excited to do their job.

Once, one of our lab technicians was helping a patient with their laboratory work, as we did every day. The patient shared with the technician their frustration with trying to get a referral to see a doctor in another facility. The technician, without prompting, took it upon herself to get all the information this patient needed. While the patient sat in the waiting room, she quickly put a plan in motion to take care of the patient's concerns. While she was taking care of the patient's business, another technician stepped in to fulfill the first tech's role at the blood drawing station.

The technician came back in 30 minutes with the patient's referral, time of her appointment, and paperwork. She took ownership of the situation and brought greater pride to our organization. I often shared that story with our newcomers to encourage them to get excited about the culture of our team and show them that they were in a position to make a difference too. It is that kind of story that builds legacy, instills pride, motivates, and encourages the team to perform at a higher quality and reliability.

Sharing how your organization is exceptional instills a sense of pride in your employees. When you tie the mission, vision, and values of the organization or department to your work and results, you instill pride. To do this, you must consistently share the stories and successes of the organization. Stories build legends, and legends build legacy, right? That legacy perpetuates the organizational pride and helps to continue the cycle of excellence.

As John Baldoni points out, "This is the part of management that requires leadership, the willingness to do what is necessary to help the team become more productive, and by extension more aware of their personal contributions. When they do, pride ensues.

Pride is essential; we want our employees to express it, but as with all things prideful, too much of it can be onerous. We call that arrogance—it turns people off. Organizations that manifest arrogance get into trouble because they overlook issues, ignore customer concerns, and even alienate employees.

Pride, on the other hand, turns people on, and that is what we want to encourage. Pride in the work is essential to fostering a more energized workplace. And when employees feel such energy they are more likely to want to come to work and do a good job. Morale improves, too, and few workplaces can do without a strong team spirit."[8]

People frequently ask me why my coworkers enjoy their jobs so much. Many clients have asked Studer Group employees about getting a job at our organization because we all seem so excited by the work we do. This a wonderful compliment for an organization.

Foster Excitement

You don't want the people that you work with to just be merely satisfied with their job. You need them to be excited and fully engaged in what they do, not only to drive greater outcomes but to attract other great talent. Let's say we're measuring employee engagement on the Likert scale – which is a five-point scale, with one being very unsatisfied and five being outstanding – four is considered satisfied. If you work for an organization where 70% of employees rated their satisfaction as a four and 30% rated as a five, that would mean 100% were satisfied with their job. At another organization, 30% of employees rated their satisfaction as a four and 70% as a five, or outstanding, that still equals 100% also, correct? Which company would you want to work for? Each has 100% satisfaction, but at organization two over 70% of the people considered it to be an outstanding place to work. What's the difference? Excitement. Engagement. Fulfillment.

Do you have fun at work? If you don't, why not? People often think that because I've worked in a military environment that my work style is rigidly disciplined. In most respects, it is. But, people are people no matter what organization or team they are a part of. People in the military have the same feelings and are motivated in the same manner as civilians. If we can have fun, you can have fun. And why shouldn't we have fun at work?

I love to share stories of the fun things we would do in the places that I was stationed over the years. In the laboratories where I worked, we used sponge balls for people to grip so that we could find a vein to draw their blood. Every now and then, our team would grab a box of them, bring everybody to the back of the lab, and have a sponge ball fight. It was simple fun, no one was hurt, and it relieved stress and tension. I also kept a squirt gun at my desk and would squirt passersby every now and then. You're probably thinking, "This guy is crazy!" You're right! I'm crazy about people enjoying their jobs and getting excited about what they do. To get people excited, you have to be excited.

The Wright brothers achieved one of humanity's most amazing accomplishments; they flew the first airplane. For years, these two men designed and made bicycles for living. They experienced failure after failure trying to get those bicycles to fly, but they stuck with it because they had a great time in the process. Wilbur Wright once said, "When my brother and I began experimenting with flight it was purely for the pleasure of it." They enjoyed what they did, and the accomplishment from that was human flight.

Think about the people you work with and the potential that lies within them. Find out what gets them excited at work and let them run with it. As a clinical laboratory manager, I managed people, data, and information related to diagnostic healthcare. I loved my job, I loved the people I worked with, and I did my job well. But I'm really passionate about value and excitement in the workplace and in our lives, as evident within the pages of this book and what I speak about all over the country. Enthusiasm breeds enthusiasm and excitement breeds excitement. Get excited about what you do and then let that excitement loose on the people you work with. It will be contagious!

In the words of Michael Josephson, "What will matter is not what you bought, but what you built, not what you got, but what you gave. What will matter is not your success, but your significance. What will matter is not what you learned, but what you taught. What will matter is every act of integrity, compassion, courage, or sacrifice that enriched, empowered or encouraged others to emulate your example. What will matter is not your competence, but your character. What will matter is not how many people you knew, but how many will feel a lasting impression when you're gone. Living a life that matters doesn't happen by accident. It's not a matter of circumstance but of choice." Choose to live a life that matters. Live a legacy.

List ways you like to feel valued, what excites you about what you do, what gives you a sense of pride:

_____

_____

_____

_____

_____

Now, think about those items and list three ways you will use those to instill value, pride, and excitement to your team, colleagues, or family.

_____

_____

_____

_____

A successful person is one who can lay a firm
foundation with the bricks that others throw
at him or her.

– David Brinkley

6

Analyze the Competition:
Look for Opportunities
to Gain the Advantage

I watched the coach between plays tell the server where to place the ball. I watched the setter analyze the defense to determine where the next ball was to be set for the next kill. Every player on the court has to know the responsibility of every other player. This leads to an increased awareness, including what happens on the other side of the net. For example, the middle blocker has the primary responsibility to block the hit from the other side. In order to do her job most effectively, she has to analyze their footwork, actions, and their motions to their teammates. If all six players understand their responsibilities and look for opportunities to score, they will always win the game. Maximizing everyone's specialty in their position will result in a dynamic and cohesive team. It ensures that no one is confused about their role.

What makes teams or organizations successful? They analyze competitive advantages to bring back to their organization that will increase productivity, job excitement, the bottom line, and financial gain. They also bring an increased competitive advantage to the team. Remember, your goal as a leader is to be a problem solver and navigate the future for your organization. To do that, you must be willing to go outside of yourself, or outside of your environment, to learn how to achieve success.

In my research, it has amazed me how company after company, team after team, and organization after organization failed to apply simple success strategies that worked for their competitors. When our Air Force service excellence team first started, we looked to Baptist Hospital in Pensacola, Florida, and later to my current employer, Studer Group, to better understand how other healthcare organizations in our area were performing. Both organizations were practically our neighbors and had excellent results. Baptist Hospital had been the number three hospital in a two-hospital town in the mid-90s, which simply means there was no need for three hospitals with the population that existed. They were dead last in patient and job satisfaction, until Baptist Hospital made changes that they sustained for years. These changes earned them the coveted Malcolm Baldridge Award in 2002. So, our service excellence team went for a visit.

We wanted to find out what they were doing to make a difference and how we could use some of those same ideas to change our organization. We took our entire team of twelve and spent two days with the Baptist team. At the end of our time with them, we had written down over thirty ideas. We then came together as a group and analyzed those ideas to determine our top ten. We took those ten and modified them to a military environment. By analyzing our 'competition", we poised ourselves to potentially evolve into one of the top medical treatment facilities in the Air Force. We were able to increase patient and staff satisfaction. Two years later, we competed for one of the highest quality awards in the Air Force and sent all twelve of our team members to Washington, D.C. to compete and tell our story.

When I was first put in a position of leadership in the military, the first thing I did was to seek out other officers in similar situations or positions. We formed a network to help each other, harvest best practices, and gain an advantage. We knew that no one person had all the answers, but collectively we had many. I still network with some of those leaders today, even though my military service has ended. Those partnerships provoke new thought, shared insights, and encouragement toward success.

Step out of your comfort zone and enter the impact zone. Look beyond yourself and find others to inspire you to greater success. "Turned *on* people figure out how to beat the competition. Turned *off* people only complain about being beaten by the competition," said author Ben Simonton.

I once read a story about Mark Victor Hansen, creator of the *Chicken Soup for the Soul* book series. Years before his great success, Hansen approached motivational speaker Tony Robbins at an event where they were both speaking. Hansen said to Tony, "I've been doing this for a long time and I'm doing okay. I'm making about $1 million a year, but I know for a fact that you are making $150 million a year with your speaking and products. How do you do it, and how can I?" Tony asked, "Who is your mastermind group (your peer mentoring group)?" Hinson replied, "They're all millionaires." "That's what you're doing wrong," Robbins remarked. "You need to find some billionaires and begin associating with them. They'll get you to the next level." If you remember, earlier in this book I said that I truly believe that God will always bring someone into your life who has been where you want to go to help you get there. Don't be afraid of the competition; learn from the competition. Learn from others to help you set up your team for success.

My son played football for the University of South Alabama where he was a wide receiver. When they practiced, he liked to line up against the best defensive player. He knew that he wasn't going to make the right move and blow past that defensive back every time, but he chose to line up against the best one so that he could become better.

It doesn't matter whether you're the leader or the manager, the employee and even the newest hire; you can analyze the competition to help your team win. Be the agent of change and find ways to make a difference, make a change, or make things right. We must continually be relentless in our pursuit of excellence. Companies and organizations around the world spend billions of dollars bringing in consultants and coaches to help them gain advantages. **Not paying attention to your peers could mean your organization is left behind or caught off guard when you should have been taking proactive measures to differentiate your business.** Conversely, an unhealthy obsession with competitive analysis may slow innovation or paralyze you from taking needed action. If you want the strategic advantage for promotion or recognition, stand out by knowing the competition.

Identify Your Competition

Some people get nervous when new people join an organization. They worry they'll lose their job or their position. But fear will keep you from performing at your best.

It can be intimidating for a volleyball player who is 5'10" to line up on the other side of the net from a competitor who is 6'3". Still, the shorter player can analyze the competition and determine the way to defeat them. How do you do that in your role?

Know who your competitors are. Are they organizations that sell or produce what you do? Are they the teams in your division or conference? If you are in the restaurant business and you specialize in pizza, is your only competition the big chain restaurants, or is every restaurant in the area in direct competition with your business? Yes, they are all in competition. If you work in a hospital, the organizations that are marketing clinical services are your competitors. CVS, Walgreens, Amazon, and Walmart are all in competition for your business. Just because they don't have capability to do surgery does not mean they are not drawing outpatient business away from you.

If you've ever watched the TV show *NCIS*, you know about Gibbs' rules. Rule #35 is, "Always watch the watchers." What that means on the show is while at a crime scene, always see who is watching what you are doing because the criminal is always there watching, too. Are you watching what your employees or team are watching? Are you paying attention to the competition? What do you see?

Do the research. It's pretty easy in sports to know who the opponent is, they have the other color jersey on, but it's not always as simple in other industries. You must define your market area, catchment area, and district. Use tools and resources online to find out who's out there taking away, or trying to take away, your business or your employees. Ask others what they know about the area, who they have seen, where they shop, etc. Do the work, don't assume.

Identify What They Are Doing

What does your competition offer that you don't? What is their competitive advantage? Remember, you need to know where you are going to know how to get there. You need to know about your opponent to know how to beat them. Are they selling the same product you are? Are they delivering, while you only offer takeout? What about their online presence? Are they using Twitter, Facebook, Instagram, online orders, or free shipping? Do they have a blog or a vlog? Sports teams look at film to watch how the other teams play, who their players are, how tall, how fast, etc. They watch them in person.

When my wife and I traveled with our daughters' volleyball teams, we spent a fair amount of time watching the other teams play while between matches. Our daughters and their teammates would analyze how the other teams played so they could learn how to gain the advantage to beat them.

In the military world, knowing how the enemy operates and what they are up to is the foremost thing to monitor to increase our advantage in defense of liberty. You cannot protect against an attack if you are not aware of what the enemy is doing. In civilian life, I realize your competitor is not necessarily the enemy. In healthcare, you are in competition for the right to take care of patients.

Countless business journals and magazines relay information about companies, their progress, and who is setting the standard in employee participation. Right now, the generation of young people entering the workforce are looking for something totally different than that of their predecessors. Millennials, those born after 1983 and before 1996, are, in the opinion of many, the most diverse generation in US history. According to a Harris poll, over 97% said that it's important to do work that allows them to have an impact on the world.[1] These new workers are not egocentric, but rather focused on self-development and aware of what they do and how it affects others. **If you are not analyzing the competition, I can tell you, they are.**

Analyze Their Strengths

Knowing the strength of the competition is key to finding your competitive advantage. What are the points of strength that the opponent possesses? Are they taller, bigger, or faster? Do they run plays that you have never seen before? When our daughter's teams would practice, part of the team would play one side of the net as if they were the other team running similar plays. This gave them an advantage to be able to know who to defend.

In business, how the other team runs their business, provides bonuses or benefits to their employees, offers discounts on merchandise, and advertises their specials will tell you how strong they are. We spy on other countries to ensure we know their strengths. We analyze satellite data, take photos, and read online chatter to keep our country safe.

I do a lot of teaching about generational differences in the workplace, and not for the reason you may think. I am often asked how to "deal with" people in other generations. I don't view it this way. I look for, and teach, the similarities and the strengths. One thing is for sure about Millennials, they are high achievers. Now, understand, I don't assume that everyone born in this generation is this way but, statistically, they are. Millennials tend to have higher expectations than any generation before them. They want *you* to be a strong leader. They expect to be treated respectfully and given opportunities to learn. Remember the environment we talked about earlier? These new workers want to have fun at work, they want to have friends, and they want a life outside of work. They are very keen on time management, because their lives have been structured from the day they were born. I would consider this to be a strength.

Most notably, Millennials want their careers to be a revolving door. This means they are going to continually be looking at the competition and what they have to offer. If you want to keep things old school, you probably won't attract – nor will you keep – this generation of workers. Each generation gives your workplace a diverse list of strengths and shortcomings. We, as leaders, must understand which strengths will overcome which weaknesses.

Analyze Their Weaknesses

A friend recently told me a story of a golfer on a pro tour. He was a pompous egomaniac with the emotional maturity of a six-year-old. He was never wrong and always had a quick excuse for any loss: it was a lousy course, the other golfers were cheating, or the weather was terrible. As if these faults were not enough, he was also not above hustling a few extra dollars playing amateurs in cities on the tour for $50 a hole. One day he was approached by a man wearing dark glasses and carrying a white cane who wanted to play him for $100 a hole. "I can't play you," the professional protested. "You're blind, aren't you?" "Yes, I am," replied the man. "But I was a state champion before I went blind. I think I can beat you." Now, the conceited pro had not been doing well lately and needed the money. Blind or not, if the guy was crazy enough to challenge him, why not? The egomaniac stated, "Well, all right. It's a deal. But don't say I didn't warn you. When would you like to play?" "Any night at all," replied the blind man. "Any night at all." What appears to be a weakness can sometimes be a strength in the right circumstance.

What was a weakness for the Wright brothers, turned into a strength with a change in circumstances. Wilbur and Orville desperately studied the variables to make their flying machine fly, they knew they couldn't stay in Dayton, Ohio. They contacted the U.S. Weather Bureau, now known as the National Weather Service, and inquired about locations that could give them the right amount of wind, soft landing spots (in case of a crash), privacy, and space. They found an idyllic home in Kittyhawk, North Carolina. This area is now known as the Outer Banks and is a popular tourist and resident location, but back in 1903 it was very secluded and offered vast space. It also offered tremendous winds. These variables lifted the Wright brothers into history. The brothers analyzed the area and chose to move operations to the best location for the outcome they desired.

Back in 2013 after a meeting with Mark Zuckerberg, Evan Speigel, the CEO of Snapchat, quickly purchased the book *The Art of War* for his team. Zuckerberg had announced that developers at Facebook were working on an app that would rival Snapchat and would be launching it soon. Facebook was looking to take over a market where Snapchat had lead, but Spiegel wasn't going down without a fight.

The Art of War was written sometime in the 5th century BC by Chinese military strategist Sun Tzu. Noted for inspiring modern military and business leaders alike, The Art of War meticulously explores different aspects of war and how they affect strategy and tactics. One of the chapters talks about exploiting your enemy's weakness and avoiding their strength. "If your opponent is of choleric temper, seek to irritate him. Pretend to be weak, that he may grow arrogant."

You may think this seems a little extreme but think about the concept. What creates the advantage for you? Knowing what weakens your competition gives you an opportunity to improve. It worked for Spiegel. Not only did Facebook's app fail to meet expectations, it boosted Snapchat's publicity. In the end, Snapchat declined Facebook's offer to buy their app, saying that it wasn't strategically valuable.

Apply Your Understanding

Once you've done your homework, you should have a better idea of things you could improve and things you could do better. Be proactive about how you differentiate your services from your competitors and emphasize what your organization does better than anyone else. Build your strategy based on the information available to you and execute against it. If you don't act, nothing will change.

At Studer Group®, we are a healthcare coaching organization and the hospitals we work with outperform all other hospitals almost two to one. We're outcomes focused and results oriented. It takes a coach and good coaching to get to the next level. So, once we have analyzed the strengths and weaknesses of your competition, to learn your advantage, we use it. In addition, we employ a team of data analysts, experts in executive leadership, specific department coaches, and organizational diagnosticians to determine your competitive advantage.

I can guarantee that if you aren't analyzing your competition your employees are. **If you're not observing other organizations, finding out how they keep and retain good employees, how they reward and recognize, how they set up people for success, then you are setting up your organization for failure.** Teach your staff, team, and colleagues how to analyze the competition. Learn it together. Set your group up for success.

As Northwestern University's Dr. Philip Kotler famously said, "Poor firms ignore their competitors; average firms copy their competitors; winning firms lead their competitors." Be the leader.

What 4 things do you need to do today to better analyze the competition, and prepare your team for the win? How will you do that?

_____

_____

_____

_____

_____

The problem with communication is the
illusion that it has been accomplished.

– George Bernard Shaw

Most conversations are simply monologues
delivered in the presence of a witness.

– Margaret Millar

7

Call Them:
Communication Is the Key
to the Perfect Setup

I noticed, as the match continued, there was constant communication and feedback between the players. The coach was consistently telling the girls where to go, what to do, where to pass the ball, and where to hit the ball. The setter would continually let the hitters know who was getting the next ball. Each team member was communicating with each other and encouraging one another. During the most concentrated plays, the communication would intensify. At times, there were disagreements, but whether positive or negative, there was continual communication. The back-row passers would yell for the ball. Sometimes, the setter would call out someone if they were between her and the ball. Other times, when she couldn't get to the ball, she would call for help. It was a dance choreographed by feedback, their continual information coming and going, overcoming barriers, and arising to win.

Communication is spoken or unspoken conduct that lets other people know what you're thinking. It is an exchange of thoughts, messages, or information. As every relationship in life is built around communication, we are all given ample opportunities to practice developing effective communication skills. And yet, every organization has issues with communication. So why is communication so difficult? *I* know what I'm trying to say, so *you* must not hear me correctly. Or, is it that I'm not listening to you? Sometimes, communication between people is difficult because we've been raised or conditioned in different ways. Some personality types are better at communicating than others while some people are inherently more reticent. Others are adept at using and interpreting non-verbal cues. No matter our strength or weakness, effective communication is essential.

In my work with more than 100 organizations, I have reviewed dozens of employee engagement surveys. Typically, in terms of percentage, the lowest scoring measurements are:

- I trust my supervisor
- Senior administrators are always visible
- Communication

Communication; that's all the survey usually indicates. What does that mean? I think we have more communication than we know what to do with in most organizations. We have in-person talks, meetings, emails, text messages, calls, newsletters, etc. What I think most employees are saying, however, is we lack *effective* communication. Or, we don't communicate every message at every level.

Consider a scenario where administration sends information to directors. The directors, in turn, must deliver that message to managers and supervisors, then the managers and supervisors are responsible for communicating the information to each of their employees. In all the communication and interpretation, information is bound to be lost in translation somewhere along the way or simply forgotten. It's like a high stakes version of the telephone game where, at the beginning of the line, one person has a message and shares it with the next person and so on until the last person repeats what the first person said. It's hilarious because what's said at the beginning is something totally different from what ends up being communicated. But who's laughing when it comes to information that can affect our output, cohesion, and success? Who's laughing when patient care is affected by ineffective communication? Nobody.

Have A Plan

It's essential that your organization or team have a communication plan or flow. It may look something like this:

1. Administration decides there are three things they want all employees to know.
2. Administration communicates this information to each director in the monthly directors meeting. Those directors are instructed, specifically, to have a face-to-face conversation with each of their managers. No one should leave the meeting without understanding the three things they need to communicate.
3. Each manager is responsible for conducting and documenting a face-to-face conversation with every employee.
4. Administration, while rounding (periodic check-ins with every department), asks employees what they know about those three topics to validate the effectiveness of the communication flow.

An accountability check while rounding is a time to validate that good communication is taking place in your organization. You can then recognize managers and leaders who are fulfilling the communication mandate. Additionally, administrators and senior leaders can identify areas that lack effective communication and improve them.

During the last ten years of Red Auerbach's coaching career, the Boston Celtics won nine National Basketball Association championships, including a record eight straight titles from 1959 to 1966. Auerbach retired at age 48 and had more wins than any other coach in NBA history, with 938 victories in twenty years. He was a coaching genius and was known for spotting talent and getting the most out of his teams. Auerbach also knew a thing or two about communication. "It's not what you tell your players that counts," he once said, "it's what they hear."

Effective communication is the key ingredient to success. A complete communication cycle includes both the ability to express ourselves clearly and accurately understand the other person. Everyone, even the most gifted communicator, needs to polish their skill to communicate their thoughts and ideas to the people around them.

When I am concluding a speaking event, I incorporate an atypical tactic, compared to most speakers' presentations. I don't ask if there any questions because it often only encourage yes and no answers. As my good friend and colleague, Dr. Jeff Morris, taught me, I simply say, "What can I explain better?" If the audience does not understand what I have communicated, then it's my responsibility to ensure that they do before the end of the event. **By asking, "What can I explain better?" I am purposefully taking the responsibility upon myself if I have not communicated well.** I teach this to healthcare providers all the time because I truly believe it will revolutionize the communication flow between a nurse or physician and their patient. This change in perspective requires you to adjust the way you explain information, and it will change the way you relate to others.

Say What You Mean and Mean What You Say

Scintillate, scintillate, globule vivific
Fain would I fathom thy nature specific.
Loftily poised in the ether capacious,
Strongly resembling a gem carbonaceous.

You're probably thinking, "What?!" However, if you think about it or break out a dictionary and look up the meanings, you'll see that it's just a verbose version of *Twinkle, Twinkle, Little Star.*

Have you ever heard or said some fashion of, "I know you believe you understand what you think I said, but I'm not sure you realize that what you heard is not what I meant?" Tell people what they need to know without going into long, lengthy explanations. In the writing of this book, I've removed and clarified thousands of words, because sometimes I talk too much. If I don't feel confident about what I'm conveying or if I am having a difficult conversation, I can ramble, which leads to ineffective and uncomfortable communication. If you feel awkward let the other person know, then tell them what it is you need to say. Communication is relevant and effective when it is clearly spoken or written. Sometimes, writing and rehearsing what you want to say helps you communicate your message more effectively.

When I am communicating important information, I will often write a long email or letter to get out everything I want to say. Then, I will go back to that message and shorten it, taking out the non-essential information. I'll then rehearse the message as if I was receiving it to ensure that it will come across as intended or have another person review my words. One time, I was able to shorten an entire page to just one paragraph.

Cleveland Amory, a famous author and animal rights enthusiast, once told a story about Judge John Lowell of Boston. "One morning the judge was at breakfast, his face hidden behind the morning paper. A frightened maid tiptoed into the room and whispered something to Mrs. Lowell. The lady paled slightly, then squared her shoulders resolutely and said, 'John, the cook has burned the oatmeal and there is no more in the house. I am afraid that this morning, for the first time in 17 years, you will have to go without your oatmeal.' The judge said, without putting down his paper, 'It's all right, my dear. Frankly, I never cared much for it anyhow.'[1] The maid was afraid to tell her boss the problem. The wife was even a bit reluctant, but then simply said what needed to be told. By the judge's reaction, he also had not communicated very well in the past 17 years.

In stating what you mean and meaning what you say, you also must be assertive. Just as Mrs. Lowell resolutely prepared herself, you must also prepare for confrontational, important, or intense situations. Being assertive gives you the freedom to express yourself in a way that accurately portrays your viewpoint. In doing so, you show confidence, which will help you present your material or information in a way that others can receive it.

If someone speaks to me with confidence, I trust they know what they're talking about, and what they have to say is important, which makes me listen more intently. I am a bottom-line person; just tell me what it is you want to tell me. I am never interested in excuses and, having a short attention span, I am not much interested in the details. As Joe Friday used to say on the TV show, *Dragnet,* "Just the facts." The exception to this would be if I'm dealing with people and their emotions or family concerns. In that case, I am extremely interested in the details. Otherwise, if you're giving me a financial report, just give me the numbers. If you're giving me directions to your house, just tell me where to turn and how far to go. I don't need to know the color of every fourth house, how many trees are in the yard, or the reason the old corner store is not there anymore.

Sometimes, employees fear that expressing their true feelings about the company to the boss may endanger their job or career. They may not be comfortable or feel welcome to give constructive feedback about what they feel or see. If this sounds like your organization or team, there needs to be an atmosphere or culture change that makes staff members feel that their message is important and that they can speak without retribution. However, I am not advocating speaking ill of others or gossiping. Just as we discussed in chapter 3, the setting is important in the ability of your team to communicate with each other. When I previously led a team, I told them at every feedback session and in our monthly staff meetings that it was important that they feel comfortable telling me what's going on and how they feel. I told them that I would not use what they said against them. As a manager and leader, I needed that open communication.

Three kids were bragging about their fathers: "My dad's so smart he can talk for one hour on any subject," said the first young man. "That's nothing," said the second, "My dad's so smart he can talk for two hours on any one subject." The third one proudly stated, "My dad is so smart, he can talk for three hours and doesn't even need a subject."[2] Say what you mean and mean what you say.

Using Humor

Victor Borge, the pianist and comedian, once said, "Humor is the shortest distance between two people." Humor has been called the spice of communication. It can break down defenses and convey information in a more refreshing manner. Getting your point across humorously can sometimes be more effective than being overly serious. Using humorous stories about ourselves when transmitting difficult information can be a more relatable approach versus being "the boss". Most lecturers or motivational speakers use humor to start their discussions because it lightens up the audience and prepares them mentally to hear the message. They will continue to use it throughout their speech to instill that message. "Laughter is a tranquilizer with no side effects," said Arnold Glasgow. Humor creates harmony. It humanizes us.

In researching his book, *Health, Healing and the Amuse System: Humor as Survival Training,* Paul McGhee, PhD found that "Research examining the dynamics of humor in task-oriented meetings suggests that it can play the pivotal role in moving the group toward a consensual solution to a problem. One study examined 26 hours of videotaped meetings held by six different management groups. The meetings generally opened with a stiff, serious tone and a communication process that was sometimes complaining and sometimes adversarial. Humor during this phase (whose average length was 30 minutes) was infrequent. When it did occur, it evoked laughter from only one or two participants, partly because it focused on discontent with others' point of view. It was after this initial serious phase that—for a period of a few minutes—the pattern of joking changed into humor that caused the entire group to laugh. While the early joking emphasized the differences between people at the meeting (and was sometimes disparaging), this mid-meeting humor drew people together and led to smoother interactions as differences were discussed."[3]

Humor makes people feel comfortable, and people learn well when they are comfortable. If we are trying to teach a lesson, humor often allows others to remember the information more readily. According to Debra Korobkin, in an article entitled, *Humor in the Classroom: Considerations and Strategies*, "Shared laughter is a powerful way to reinforce learning. Humor can set students at ease and increase group rapport. Humor can also be used to compliment, to guide or to provide negative feedback in a positive manner." [4] Some of the alleged benefits of humor in a group tutorial session include increased:

- retention of material
- attentiveness and interest
- motivation towards and satisfaction with learning
- playfulness and positive attitude
- individual and group task productivity
- discussion and animation
- creativity, idea generation, and divergent thinking [5]

She goes on to say, "Not only does humor generate divergent thinking, it can also spark student recall long after the group session is over. When students and teachers were asked what element makes learning effective and exciting, a 'sense of humor' was rated high on the list. Shared laughter is a powerful way to reinforce learning." [6] The same holds true in communicating within our organizations.

AIDET

At Studer Group, we coach what we call the five fundamentals of communication. We use the acronym AIDET®, which stands for Acknowledge, Introduce, Duration, Explanation and Thank you, to teach this method for effective communication. In its simplicity, it is the easiest way to reduce anxiety and increase compliance in patients. But it works in so many arenas.

Have you ever walked up to the front desk of an establishment and it seemed as though the people working there didn't even notice you? Or, if they did look up, they gave you a look as though you were bothering them? Simple acknowledgment makes people feel valued. The fact that we *acknowledge* a person's concern or their need, or just use their name, means enough to bring value to them as a person.

What if you also *introduce* yourself, letting the person know who you are and how you can help, by saying something like, "Hello, Ms. Richer, my name is Mark, how can I assist you today?" Think about how this might affect those you interact with. Small adjustments to how you introduce yourself can change how others perceive you and make them more open to what you have to say.

Waiting, especially when not knowing how long something will take, also leads to anxiety. When we communicate the *duration* of a project, or how long a wait may be, we reduce the anxiety and concern of our employee or customer. This simple communication brings great relief and impact.

The *explanation* is one of the most important keys to communication, and yet, it is often overlooked. You may explain things in a way you understand them, but maybe not in the way a customer, patient, or co-worker understands them. Your explanation must capture the intent, content, and extent of what you most want that person to know and comprehend. Do you explain your expectations when you are delegating a project? Do you explain the process of how something works, so others might understand why it may take longer than they expect?

The *thank you* is simple. "Thank you for your time." "Thank you for choosing our business." "Thank you for being patient as I explained this." Be grateful for others, their time, and their efforts.

For more information, visit www.studergroup.com/AIDET.

Feedback

Feedback is a system or process through which people give and receive information. Both giving and receiving feedback requires an ability to listen and understand. Remember what Pat Summit, said, "In the absence of feedback, people will always fill in the blanks with a negative." That's a powerful statement when you consider how feedback affects organizational success.

Research shows the link between free-flowing feedback and better business results. In workplaces where managers don't ask for or provide feedback, employee engagement rates sank to 29%. [7] On the flip side, when feedback is encouraged between managers and employees, engagement jumps to 79%. [8]

In my military days, we received feedback at our annual evaluations, then 60 days later, and at a mid-year review. That is not nearly enough. Too much time between feedback sessions will cause many people to lose their focus on improving performance and also allows ample time to fill in the blanks with negative thoughts. If I don't hear feedback about how I am doing, I will automatically think my boss doesn't like what I am doing.

Several times a month I get feedback from my boss, which enables me to grow and become a better leader and employee. When I combine the feedback from my boss and co-workers with the feedback I receive from clients and customers, I get a full picture of where I need to improve and where I am doing well. This feedback also lets me know how far I have come and how my strengths have grown. I use this information to create a development plan for my career and my future.

To give effective feedback, you must first understand how the other person likes to receive feedback. Knowing what they value, or directly asking how they prefer to receive feedback, will reduce instances of miscommunication. When giving critical feedback, remind the recipient that you believe in them and their abilities. Once you know they've heard and understood you, remind them of the goal you are collectively trying to achieve. Ask the person to try again, using this new information, their drive for excellence, and the support of the team as inspiration.

"What would the world be like if we were speaking powerfully, to people who were listening consciously, in environments that were actually fit for purpose?" – Julian Treasure

Make today about improving your communication skills and your listening style. How will you do that?

_____

_____

_____

_____

_____

Start with what they know. Build with what
they have. The best of leaders when the job is done,
when the task is accomplished, the people will say
we have done it ourselves.

– Lao Tzu

8

Set the Right Player:
Putting the Right Person,
In the Right Place,
At the Right Time

It seemed as though she knew where every player was at any given moment of the game. The setter would watch the defense, analyze which of her players was in the right position and set the ball to them. I noticed that there were several rotations in a row where a hitter would not get the ball. The setter knew who was on their game and who wasn't. The coach knew which players should be in what position, but the setter knew who to get the ball to.

Have you ever seen a food commercial so many times that you just had to eat what they advertised? Did you go to that restaurant, order that dish, and it was just the right thing? It was exactly what you wanted. It was exactly what you needed. It was the right fit at the right time.

In any company, large or small, lies an amalgamation of talent. Each team member lends their skills and expertise to collectively make an organization. It is essential, for this organization to be the best that it can be, that everyone is in the right position for maximum impact.

Even back in Michelangelo's day, master artists hired workers for their special abilities: gilding, painting background landscapes, rendering the folds of a garment and so on. These people worked according to the master's plan and were paid accordingly. As a production model, this environment had its good points and bad points. Assigning the less technical work to apprentices allowed the master to produce much more than he might have otherwise in his lifetime but, it still placed the entire burden of success on the master. So it is with a team.

Teams need to harness the brainpower of more than one person if for no other reason than to share the workload and the victory. I see this in sports all the time; a star athlete who hates to share the glory but wants to share the labor. Each athlete on a major sports team plays a key role in the team's outcome.

Did you know human DNA code is 99% the same? [1] Even though it accounts for all the information that makes up an organism, DNA is built using only four nucleotides: adenine, guanine, thymine, and cytosine. [2] That's it. Simple right? If we can break something as complex as DNA down to its essence, why can't we find the right DNA sequence and correct neural connectors to ensure you get the best people for your team? You can't, because it isn't a scientific calculation. It really comes down to knowing people, knowing their behavior, their values, their talents. How do we do that?

We may not always have the star performers or the best talent. But, by putting people in the right place at the right time, we can still win championships or become the most productive company in the world. Putting the right people in the right place at the right time can enable even the most undervalued players to rise to the top. Each person using their gifts and talents together is a beautiful symphony of work.

Herb Brooks, the renowned coach of the 1980 US Olympic gold medal-winning hockey team once said, "I'm not looking for the best players, just the right ones." He had the right idea. The medal-round match between the United States and the Soviet Union, known as the "Miracle on Ice," is one of the most illustrious sporting conquests in US history. My favorite movie of all-time, *Miracle*, is based on this famous game. In it, Kurt Russell in his portrayal of Herb Brooks, says this great line, "The name on the front (of their jerseys) is more important than the name on the back." What he meant is that the team is more important than the individual. Greatness is not in being the strongest but in the right use of that strength.

While I will never claim that all poor performers can become superstars, I argue that their potential contribution is severely limited if they are not in the right place. In other words, high performance is partly driven by being in the right place, with the right group, at the right time. After all, aren't we talking about the setup? Isn't this the entire heart of what this book is about? **Putting people in the right place at the right time is the absolute beginning to set them up for success.**

Over the years, I have noticed that certain personalities fit certain positions. An understanding of a person's personality provides predictive tools to identify their potential before they may even know it themselves. The Big Five factors of personality – extroversion, agreeableness, conscientiousness, neuroticism, and openness to experience – can predict about 50% of the variability in leadership, with intelligence and dark side traits contributing significant additional variance. [3,4,5]

In your next team training, give personality tests to your employees to help them assess their strengths and weaknesses. Often, putting a person in the position that fits their personality will produce the best outcome for the organization and the employee. You may find that certain personalities are more detail-oriented than others. These people could be great at managing your finances or budget, ordering supplies, managing your shipping department, or any other role that requires exceptional accuracy. Still, others may not have that eye for detail. This doesn't mean that they cannot fit in your organization, it simply means they may function better in a different role.

When I put together teams, I don't always try to find people who all think alike. I try to find people who can work together. It is more important to have a team that complements each other's strengths and skills rather than a team who has all the same skills, which can lead to gaping holes in performance. You need the right people in the right job at the right time. The right person for a role in a $1 million organization may not be the right person to get you to a $1 billion business. The abilities of your creative and talented personnel create a higher demand for your product or service. This, in turn, creates a greater level of performance. Each level requires more. Each time people show themselves responsible with what they have, they qualify themselves for more.

Finding your hidden gems is not enough, you must also harness their full potential. The more sophisticated your talent identification processes are, the more "raw" your candidates will be because you spotted their potential at an earlier stage. At the same time, the earlier you start working on their development, the more they will develop.

When I am home, between trips and on the weekends, my wife and I walk our dog along the coastline of a deep-water bayou in the panhandle of Florida where we currently live. Almost every time, I witness dolphins playing very near where we walk. I never tire of watching them. I also learn lessons from them. Dolphins have amazing, innate talent – the levels of which I didn't know existed outside of captivity. I previously thought that dolphins only came out of the water and did flips when they were trained to in places like SeaWorld. I didn't know that they did this naturally until I saw a pod playing in this bayou and noticed the adults teaching the babies to do this trick.

Another time, while paddle-boarding with my wife and a friend, I saw a dolphin going backward just as you would see in a show. It would dart forward then backward, the front half of its body in the air and the back half under water. It was great to see. We were even more amazed when we noticed that the dolphin had a fish in its mouth and was flipping it in the air and catching it again. My wife and I love to follow them, trying to anticipate where they will surface when we see them take a deep breath and dive. We have observed these creatures so many times that we have learned patterns in their behavior. We've become fairly accurate, about 50% of the time, at knowing where and when they will surface from under the water, so we paddle to the point where we anticipate they will emerge from the deep.

What did I learn, other than dolphins are smart, talented, and can do tricks I didn't know about? Observation leads to proper placement. When you watch people and observe their skills, gifts, talents, and abilities, you learn where to put them and where their skills are most beneficial to the team.

For example, a technician that worked for me was very competent in the laboratory. She also loved doing fundraisers for our hospital. I saw how she handled people when for donations for charities or events. After noticing this, I looked for other opportunities for her to participate in events. Inadvertently, she excelled even more in her regular work in the lab. She felt an even greater purpose in her work because she also used her skills in other areas.

Steven DeMaio describes the advantage perfectly. "Good managers know what their individual employees like to do (what tasks they enjoy, which projects motivate them). Great managers find out *why* someone has those preferences – i.e., which project characteristics are the root sources of fulfillment. That kind of knowledge helps a manager strategically match an employee with a project, taking into account both the essence of the work and the essence of the person rather than just the category or domain where there appears to be a synergy. For example, Rosa might have enjoyed that customer-feedback project not because she likes working with surveys but because she has a strong affinity for the product that was being evaluated. Her next assignment should be related to that product, not a survey on a different product."[6]

Your responsibility as a leader is to take those natural gifts and abilities (flipping out of the water, swimming backward) and refine them so employees can perform at their highest capability on command, so to speak. It's similar to how trainers work at Sea-World, using repetition and validation to train dolphins. The goal is not for the dolphin to do the trick, but to know when and how often they should do it for the performance. Their gifts and talents are already there!

I work mostly in the healthcare industry with a variety of medical providers: physicians, nurses, nurse practitioners, physician assistants, etc. There are some very skilled medical professionals in America, but when a physician has an MD or DO license it doesn't necessarily make them good at every aspect of medicine. Similarly, just because a nurse is good in the emergency department does not mean she or he will be great in the obstetrics unit. Does that make them a bad or unskilled nurse? No, it just means they're not the right fit for that role.

When I was a laboratory scientist, I functioned well in all areas but was better in some than others. Since I often worked in the lab by myself on weekends, I had to know how to do it all. I excelled at chemistry and hematology where we tested cholesterol and blood cell counts. If you were hiring me back then, you'd definitely want me in those areas. However, if you wanted me to work exclusively as a microbiologist – those that work with bacteria – I may not have been the best fit. I previously mentioned that I am in my third role with Studer Group. I fit in my first team, I fit better in the next, and now I fit very well fulfilling my lifelong passion of impacting leaders by speaking, writing, and teaching.

The highest performers in your department may not always be the people you most suspect. Try asking each member of your team what they are passionate about, and if allowed, what they would really want to do in their role. Mix it up a little in your office or organization by putting somebody in a different place and seeing what they can do. You might be surprised to see people excel in areas you didn't hire them for. **Accomplishments of the greatest magnitude only happen when we step out of the comfort zone we have established for ourselves and others.** This is the number one thing you can do to set up the next leader for success. In the wise words of Mother

Teresa, "You can do what I cannot do. I can do what you cannot do. Together we can do great things."

1. Have a conversation with your staff members and ask what they are good at and what they would like to do, if given the opportunity.

_____

_____

_____

_____

_____

2. Have each member of your team take a personality test. Discuss their strengths and traits.

_____

_____

_____

_____

_____

Patience and perseverance have a magical
effect before which difficulties disappear
and obstacles vanish.

– John Quincy Adams

9

Play It Off the Net:
Patience is Passion Tamed

As the setter passed the ball, it went into the net. She tried to reach it, but the ball fell to the ground before her hands could touch it. The next time the ball went in the net, the setter dove for it, only to fall out of bounds. The coach pulled the setter aside and gave her some direction. The next time the ball went into the net, the setter positioned herself, waited for the ball to pop off the net, then set it to the outside hitter. What did the coach tell her? "Just be patient." The coach advised her how to position herself under the net, bend her knees, and crouch down to wait for the ball to meet her. By keeping an eye on the net and where it makes contact, the setter would know whether the ball would roll down the net or bounce off it. She had to be patient and ready to react and move, dependent upon where the ball hit.

The preacher, Philip Brooks, was noted for his poise and quiet manner. As with most people, even he suffered moments of frustration and irritability. One day, a friend saw him pacing like a caged lion. "What's the trouble, Mr. Brooks?" he asked. Brooks replied, "The trouble is I'm in a hurry, but God isn't!" Truth be told, we're all in a hurry. There is a song by the band Alabama that proclaims in the lyrics, "I'm in a hurry and don't know why." It resonates so much with me. Leonardo da Vinci is quoted as saying, "Patience serves as a protection against wrongs, as clothes do against cold. People put on more clothes as the cold increases so the cold will have no power to hurt them. So, in a like manner, you must grow in patience when you meet with great wrongs."

What does patience have to do with setting up yourself and others for successful leadership? As illustrated above, the setter cannot set up the hitter without being patient. If she rushes to get the ball, she will only cause the ball to go out of bounds or fall to the floor. Her patience is essential to the success of the team. If you have a pear tree, what happens if you cut it down to get the pears, rather than picking them? You get pears for the moment, but your eagerness destroys the future growth.

In an attempt to gain success quickly, we sometimes get ahead of ourselves and rush through the learning process, diminishing or risking an opportunity. Though we are passionate about the opportunity, we can lose sight of the path to victory. Passion untamed can cause impatience. Impatience robs us of happiness while patience reaps the reward of happiness. Of course, this takes practice and effort; what is worthwhile in life that doesn't? **Patience delivers success when teamed with perseverance. You can't have one without the other.**

Patience is the capacity for calmly enduring difficult situations. [1] It is the ability to wait for something without complaining or giving up. Patience is good-natured tolerance or a cheerful obliging disposition.

Similarly, the dictionary defines perseverance as the continued effort to do or achieve something despite difficulties, failure, or opposition. [2] So, when we define patience in our own lives, we must define it not by if, but rather by how, we wait for things. And with what diligence? Are we calm, even cheerful, as we wait? This simple measurement differentiates patience versus endurance. With endurance, we are just waiting it out, hoping for a good outcome. With patience, we are peacefully waiting to see what happens. Patience alongside perseverance yields the promise of pursuit.

If you are a good cook, you know what patience is. I am not a good cook. In fact, let's just say, I am not a cook at all. I once ate a soggy pizza that I heated in the microwave in five minutes because I didn't want to wait for the oven. On the other hand, my wife is a fantastic cook. She loves to cook and has the patience, desire, and perseverance to do what is necessary to eat well. Through her, I have learned to be more patient because the reward is worth it.

The military is good at developing patience in its troops. Those of us who have served are experts at the practice of "hurry up and wait." The government gives a deadline for something to get done, and we do it. Then we wait for the government to act on it. And wait, and wait, and wait. In basic training, we would march to an appointment, sometimes arriving hours ahead of time, only to sit and wait for our turn.

When I was a teen, I spent ten weeks along the Amazon River in Brazil. It was a missionary trip to build a new school for the kids of local missionaries. To build the schoolhouse, we had to move, quite literally, a mountain of dirt. We dug out the hillside which was 25 feet wide and more than 40 feet deep. Additionally, the tallest peak on this hill was more than 12 feet high, equating to 12,000 cubic feet of dirt. We did this with nothing more than shovels, pickaxes, and wheelbarrows. It took us more than three weeks of digging and hauling dirt to move all that material. That is perseverance. I gained my fair share of patience on that trip.

In competitive play, calm under fire usually comes with experience. The volleyball player who gets frustrated, blows up or pulls mental blunders loses close games for the team. Though a sense of calm is not only seen in the setter, it seems to be accentuated in that position.

My daughter, Hannah, is a great example of this. Sometimes, she seems emotionless on the volleyball court. But her calm cures her team's nervousness and settles them so they can play more effectively. Her steadfastness motivates them and interestingly, shows the rest of the team that they can produce great results. Calmness under fire is the stabilizing factor in any highly emotional person with a competitive spirit, in contrast to a smart player who lets the closeness of the game affect their thinking.

Slow Down

Sometimes we just need to *slow down*. Must we do everything in a rush? Unless you are an emergency department staff member and an ambulance is approaching, you may not need to rush. Certainly, I am asking the man in the mirror, because I sometimes have little patience. When I am eating with my family or a group of people, I purposely slow myself down and consciously think about each bite. Why? For years, I have eaten like my food was going to be taken away. People have told me they get anxious when eating with me because of how fast I clean my plate.

Similarly, when I am speaking in front of a group, I must consciously slow myself down at times. I tend to get very excited about what I teach, which causes me to speak faster. But, in doing so, I may lose the attention of the audience. So I slow down, breathe, and use intentional pauses to keep the audience's focus.

A story about an NYC Taxi driver made me think about how, by rushing through much of my time, I miss out on things that are truly important:

I arrived at the address and honked the horn. After waiting a few minutes, I honked again. Since this was going to be my last ride of my shift I thought about just driving away, but instead I put the car in park and walked up to the door and knocked. "Just a minute," answered a frail, elderly voice. I could hear something being dragged across the floor.

After a long pause, the door opened. A small woman in her nineties stood before me. She was wearing a print dress and a pillbox hat with a veil pinned on it, like somebody out of a movie from the 1940s.

By her side was a small nylon suitcase. The apartment looked as if no one had lived in it for years. All the furniture was covered with sheets. There were no clocks on the walls, no knickknacks or utensils on the counters. In the corner was a cardboard box filled with photos and glassware.

"Would you carry my bag out to the car?" she said. I took the suitcase to the cab, then returned to assist the woman. She took my arm and we walked slowly toward the curb. She kept thanking me for my kindness. "It's nothing," I told her. "I just try to treat my passengers the way I would want my mother to be treated." "Oh, you're such a good boy," she said. When we got in the cab, she gave me an address and then asked, "Could you drive through down-town?" "It's not the shortest way," I answered quickly. "Oh, I don't mind," she said. "I'm in no hurry. I'm on my way to a hospice." I looked in the rear-view mirror. Her eyes were glistening. "I don't have any family left," she continued in a soft voice. "'The doctor says I don't have very long.'" I quietly reached over and shut off the meter. "What route would you like me to take?" I asked.

For the next two hours, we drove through the city. She showed me the building where she had once worked as an elevator operator. We drove through the neighborhood where she and her husband had lived when they were newlyweds. She had me pull up in front of a furniture warehouse that had once been a ballroom where she had gone dancing as a girl.

As the first hint of sun was creasing the horizon, she suddenly said, "I'm tired. Let's go now." We drove in silence to the address she had given me. It was a low building, like a small convalescent home, with a driveway that passed under a portico. Two orderlies came out to the cab as soon as we pulled up. They were solicitous and intent, watching her every move. They must have been expecting her. I opened the trunk and took the small suitcase to the door. The woman was already seated in a wheelchair.

"How much do I owe you?" She asked, reaching into her purse. "Nothing," I said. "You have to make a living," she answered. "There are other passengers," I responded. Almost without thinking, I bent and gave her a hug. She held onto me tightly. "You gave an old woman a little moment of joy," she said. "Thank you." I squeezed her hand, and then walked into the dim morning light. Behind me, a door shut. It was the sound of the closing of a life.

I didn't pick up any more passengers that shift. I drove aimlessly lost in thought. For the rest of that day, I could hardly talk. What if that woman had gotten an angry driver, or one who was impatient to end his shift? What if I had refused to take the run, or had honked once, then driven away? On a quick review, I don't think that I have done anything more important in my life.

Slow down, enjoy the journey.

Five Second Pause

When in doubt, insert a two to five-second pause before answering a question, responding to an occurrence, or reacting to a situation. Five seconds can seem like an eternity, but it isn't, and it works. Living life in the present and being mindful of others will help you slow down. Learning to pause means listening and thinking before opening your mouth. In the few seconds of a pause, you may realize how to be more effective in what you say, determine it doesn't need to be said at all or allow your counterpart to process your viewpoint.

When speaking, the power of the pause gives your audience time to process the information and encourages attentiveness. "Taking a two-second pause can make you more approachable," says career expert, Jeff Black, "since preventing others from finishing their thoughts typically comes off as abrasive. When you consciously slow down your actions and speech in the office, you seem more comfortable and have more time to think through your next move."

He continues, "An important caveat: You shouldn't slow down to the point of being monotone and boring, but you should think before you speak. Taking a pause helps you to be more thoughtful and engaged, which is especially important if you are leading a team.

Part of being a good leader is knowing when to be quiet and listen. Even if you have made your decision and they are presenting the different strategies, you should have the respect for your team to be quiet. When you listen and take a beat before responding, you appear more open-minded and measured, which in turn makes people more likely to listen to what you have to say."[3]

Read

Read voraciously! Not only does reading slow you down, it improves your focus, and makes you a smarter and more interesting person and leader. The more you stimulate your mind, the more creative and versatile you become. Reading keeps you ahead of your peers and sets you to make good decisions. In a recent *Inc.* article, writer Brian Evans stated that top CEOs in America read 4-5 books a month.[4] It could be argued that top executive leaders likely read more than anyone else in their organizations. These are the game changers in corporate America. I read at least one book and listen to one audiobook a month, with a combined goal of 25 per year.

The more you read, the more patience you acquire. What we require of ourselves, we will eventually acquire in ourselves. Don't just read the headline or the first paragraph; read it all, front to back.

Make Yourself Uncomfortable

Change your routine. Whatever you usually do first, instead, do it second or third. Get dressed in a different order. Take a different route in your commute. Changing your routine is an excellent practice in patience because it requires you to be more present. Routine helps you feel in control and, in my opinion, long-term control inevitably dulls your senses.

When my oldest daughter, Bailey, was a junior in high school, she decided she wanted to play Division 1 college volleyball. She knew her goal would require her to step up her game. So, she moved out of her comfort zone and joined another club's volleyball team. You see, she had played volleyball with the same girls for the past five years, but to be ready for collegiate volleyball she needed to challenge herself differently. Bailey's new routine included driving 60 miles twice a week to Panama City, Florida to play with a club team composed of girls who also played for her high school team's archrivals. This was uncomfortable, but she did it, and she grew, eventually earning her spot on her college team.

In her article, *Discomfort Is What You Feel When You're Growing*, author Tasha Eurich says, "Even the act of being uncomfortable can be a reward in and of itself. New situations trigger a unique part of our mid-brain that then releases dopamine, one of nature's feel-good chemicals. But here's what's interesting: this region of the brain is only activated when we see or experience *completely* new things. Some examples:
- Putting yourself in a totally new situation.
- Making new connections (like joining a new club or sitting at a different lunch table).
- Disregarding what others think of you (like dining alone or dancing with reckless abandon).
- Breaking a habit by trying something new (like taking a different tactic with a problem employee).
- Taking a risk (like suggesting a new idea at work or asking someone on a date)."[5]

This will certainly create more patience in and around you.

My good friend Rich Bluni often says, "Get comfortable with being uncomfortable." It is one of the keys to developing patience.

Talk to Yourself

Sometimes, you just need to tell yourself to be patient. In other words, it's better to talk to yourself than to listen to yourself.

There's a story of a man who observed a woman in the grocery store with a three-year-old girl in her cart. As they passed the cookie section, the little girl asked for cookies and her mother told her no. The little girl immediately began to whine and fuss. The mother said quietly, "Now Monica, we only have half of the aisles left to go through; don't be upset. It won't be long." Soon, they came to the candy aisle and the little girl began to shout for candy. And when she was told she couldn't have any, she began to cry. The mother said, "There, there, Monica. Only two more aisles to go, and then we'll be checking out." When they got to the check-out stand, the little girl immediately began to clamor for gum and burst into a terrible tantrum upon discovering there would be no gum purchased. The mother patiently said, "Monica, we'll be through in five minutes and then you can go home and have a nice nap." The man followed the mother and child out to the parking lot and stopped the woman to compliment her. "I couldn't help noticing how patient you were with little Monica," he said. Whereupon the mother said, "*I'm* Monica; my little girl's name is Tammy." Sometimes, we have to talk our way into patience.

If you want to be the setter, the leader, then patience is an absolute. The same goes when leading people. We position ourselves with others to help propel them and set them in the right spot. We patiently anticipate where the ball is going to hit the net, so we know best how to set the player. We patiently watch the people we work with to see how challenges will bounce off them, to help us determine how to support them. Just as the teacher must have patience with the student, or the coach must have patience with the team, the boss must have patience with the employee. Knowing them and their skills, strengths, and talents will help you patiently lead them.

My son, Taylor, loves to play sports. He has coached soccer and basketball and taught other sports. Many weekends, we watched him with some of the neighborhood kids as he patiently instructed them on how to run routes, make plays, and throw, pass, and shoot a ball. He had a passion for the game and, in the midst of that passion, had the patience to teach others.

Lester Lewis Brown once stated, "A dream can be nurtured over years and years and then flourish rapidly. Be patient. It will happen for you. Sooner or later, life will get weary of beating on you and holding the door shut on you and then it will open and throw you a real party!" Any of you who have ever dreamed of becoming something or envisioned an accomplishment knows what it is like to be patient. As the old adage goes, "A boxing champion is not made in the ring, he is only recognized there." Years of preparation will yield moments of glory. Patience is a necessary ingredient of genius, a necessary component in grit, a necessary element of parenting, and necessary portion of leadership.

In the early years of our marriage, my wife and I were like most young couples. We wanted more than we can afford and didn't have enough patience to save money to buy those things. We wanted furnishings for our house so, rather than saving money to buy something of quality, we bought cheap particle board furniture. As you know, particle board tends to fall apart quicker than solidly built furniture. In our endeavor to gain, we lost in the long run. Our impatience only cost us more over time. As we grew and learned, we realized that if we wanted to purchase things that would last for a long time we had to be patient and save our money.

In the mid 1800's, the American poet, Josiah Gilbert Holland, so eloquently stated, "Let this be understood, then, at starting; that the patient conquest of difficulties which rise in the regular and legitimate channels of business and enterprise is not only essential in securing the success which you seek, but it is essential to that preparation of your mind, requisite for the enjoyment of your successes, and for retaining them when gained. So, day by day, and week by week; month after month, and year after year, work on, and in that process gain strength and symmetry, and nerve and knowledge, that when success, patiently and bravely worked for, shall come, it may find you prepared to receive it and keep it."[6] I appreciate immensely how articulate he is in this message. People don't speak like that anymore; they just don't have the patience to do it.

What steps are you going to take today to become more patient?

_____

_____

_____

_____

Surround yourself with the best people you can find,

delegate authority, and don't interfere.

– Ronald Reagan

10

Delegate It or Do It:
Know When to Hold 'Em,
Know When to Fold 'Em

As the pace of the game increased, I watched the setter run from side to side, doing all she could. I also noticed when she would yell to another player to get the ball. She knew she couldn't make it in time, so she delegated the responsibility of the set to someone else. A good setter knows when they can make it to the ball and when they need help. It all comes down to effective teamwork. Each player has a responsibility yet knows when to ask for help.

The job of the manager, leader, or coach is to get results by guiding and leading other people. When you delegate responsibility or authority, you transfer that work to the other person, but you also transfer some accountability. It cannot be overstated that delegation is the most important ability that successful leaders demonstrate. It is also the most needed and, unfortunately, the most underused.

Delegation is to entrust another person with the power or authority to act. The key word here is trust. For many managers and leaders, coaches or players, it is difficult to let go and let other people take care of your business. After all, you earned a position of leadership because you know how to take care of business. You know how to get things done. In reality, it is selfish to not trust your team to act. When you don't give others an opportunity or responsibility, it shows you are primarily concerned with your own agenda.

The word trust means to have assured reliance on the character, ability, strength, or truth of someone or something.[1] How sad it is to be in such a state of mind as to not be able to trust. If you cannot trust your team, you are inherently saying that you are the only one who can make that event happen or accomplish whatever task needs to be done. You have likely heard the saying, "If you want something done right, do it yourself." It couldn't be more wrong. I cannot overemphasize how important it is to trust others.

I've heard it said, "I would rather have 100 people doing the work than doing the work of 100 people." Some managers and leaders never learn how to delegate. Fortunately, early in my career, I learned the art of delegation. Many of my colleagues jokingly said that I was lazy, but I knew that to be an effective manager, or better yet, an effective leader, I would have to delegate some responsibilities. Sometimes you do it, sometimes you delegate it.

Leaders who don't delegate are hoarders. I tell leaders all the time that they tend to hoard responsibility and work. And in healthcare, especially, they tend to be very concerned about how much workload is being put on staff and work too hard on things they should delegate. Most leaders work very hard, and they should, but they work harder than they need to because they don't know how or refuse to delegate. Imagine a scenario where a hard-working, phenomenal nurse becomes a nurse manager or leader. Once they find work that needs to be done, they do it themselves rather than delegating it to their staff. This is why I call them hoarders. They may think, "I don't want to burden my nurses, they are busy enough," or "I need this done now, so I might as well take care of it." So, instead of delegating those tasks, they hoard them. Hoarding work robs staff of opportunities to learn and grow, and also overburdens the leader. The art of delegation is a learned behavior that starts with trust.

Delegation Is Trust

In 1850, a man named Charles Blondin crossed Niagara Falls on a tightrope. It must have taken nerves of steel to accomplish something like that, knowing that falling would surely mean death. Nevertheless, he completed the stunt several times. He crossed blindfolded, once with a wheelbarrow, and another time on stilts. But, in 1859 he performed one of his most incredible feats when he crossed the falls on a tightrope, carrying a man on his back. Can you imagine what that must have been like for that man? That is trust. Trust and delegation are learned behaviors.

Trust begins with understanding ourselves. A foundation of trusting yourself and knowing your vision allows you to trust others. Trust starts very small, and when others are found to be trustworthy leads us to enlarge the opportunities for others, leading to greater trust. Consistent feedback to the person with whom you are building trust is essential, and that feedback needs to come from all involved.

Trust continues with your commitment to be available, but not interfere unless requested. The expectation of when a responsibility should take place and be completed must be communicated. This may sound like, "Mark, I need you to complete this research for me by Friday at 11:00 a.m. If you need me, I will be in the office all week and available to answer your questions. This is a priority project, but I will not interfere unless you need me."

Leadership is not difficult. I don't say that without a bit of reservation because it can be difficult for some. But ultimately, a leader is charged with the task of helping a group of people accomplish a goal. The leader does not have to be the sole decision-maker; they don't have to have all the answers. Delegating responsibility enables the group to reach a goal. If decision making is not delegated, or cannot be delegated, then often the implementation of those decisions is delegated.

Gone are the days when a company relies on the knowledge, wisdom, and problem-solving skills of just one person, the boss. While experience and knowledge are incredibly valuable, knowledge must be shared for an organization to reach its goals. The delegator (leader) needs to focus on what the delegate has to offer and how a task is suited to their talent, personality, or skill. When looking for the person to delegate to, leaders must look at how it will benefit the person and the organization; one is not more important than the other. Also, ask the delegate if this task is something they want to do and if they think it will help them grow.

Leadership styles are often situational. Depending on your own capabilities, your staff's capabilities, or the task at hand, varying degrees of delegation may be appropriate. Much of the effectiveness will rely on the individual and distinctive personality of the delegator. You must know yourself, your strengths, and know when to delegate what you cannot accomplish. In addition, knowing your team, their strengths and desires will help you to know whom and where to delegate.

Some of the degrees of delegation are:

- **Limited delegation:** Delegate specific tasks to new hires based on the experience. This requires more oversight, check-ins, and opportunities for questions.
- **Moderate delegation:** Experienced employees can be given tasks that are a little outside of their comfort zone, but they have the trust of the leader and the critical thinking, decision making, and project management skills to get the job done.
- **Full delegation:** Having delegated a project or task, a leader can have full confidence that it will be completed by the designated deadline with little additional input or intervention.

As I mentioned earlier, whenever I sat down for feedback with my team, I let them know that I would delegate a great amount of responsibility to them. I told them that I would stretch them beyond what they thought they were capable of doing and that I would never give more than I thought they could handle. I also emphasized that they needed to let me know if they felt I had given them more than they could handle. Have you ever held a rubber band in your hands and began to stretch it? Just when you think it's going to break, it stretches more. That is what I teach others about their abilities; I will do my best to ensure they don't break but rather help them to fully stretch. In fact, once a rubber band is stretched the first time, it never returns to its same, smaller size, which isn't dissimilar to people as they grow.

During my early years as a laboratory manager, one of my best lab technicians came to me almost in tears. He felt as though I had delegated too much to him. I knew he was able to handle a lot, but in my eagerness to help him grow I had put too much on him. He was one of the best technicians and I knew could count on him to complete projects with great results. But I learned that he could only handle so much and that his attention to detail was best suited for giving him projects one at a time. Fortunately, for him and for me, he knew I was approachable and he felt comfortable communicating his frustrations. Later he thanked me for how I both pushed him and communicated with him. And, he has since attained the highest rank in the Air Force and daily leads hundreds of staff in one of the largest medical facilities in the military.

When delegating, it's important to ensure that your team is learning proper time management skills. **Giving your team tasks and expecting them to know inherently how**

to manage their time is poor leadership. Many times, I have listened to others tell me how busy they are, how much work they have to do, and how little time they have. I even had a co-worker, many years ago, list all her tasks each day just so I could see how busy she was. It took her more time to list them than do them. "Those who make the worst use of their time are the first to complain of its shortness," says 17th century French essayist, Jean de la Bruyere.

General George Patton said, "Never tell people how to do things. Tell them what to do and they will surprise you with their ingenuity." I love the way the former secretary of defense Donald Rumsfeld talks about delegation. He said, "Don't be a bottleneck. If a matter is not a decision for the president or you, delegate. Force responsibility down and out. Find problem areas, add structure and delegate. The pressure is to do the reverse. Resist it." While it's simple to say, delegating may not always be easy to do. When in doubt, route.

Delegation Increases Motivation

Delegating work to staff members increases their motivation. In an organization with a culture of teamwork, everyone knows that they're all in it together. A deep feeling of personal involvement and investment will pay dividends for job satisfaction and increase productivity. If organizations share a common vision, delegate responsibilities and authority, and work together as a team, the synergy will create a highly effective, highly engaged machine.

Why is it hard for many managers and leaders to delegate work? How else can you train future leaders if you don't delegate responsibility to them? Many managers talk about delegation and yet try to do everything themselves or they feel a need to be in the limelight and want others to know that they do everything by themselves. Still, others assign responsibility without any autonomy. When you insist on handling all the details and work yourself, you are ultimately working yourself into health problems or the grave.

Give Responsibility

Sharing responsibility for the work that's done in your organization keeps your staff excited and interested in the success of the organization. It gives them ownership. When the setter on a volleyball team gives the opportunity to other players to help her out, it increases the success of the team. She's not running herself ragged and can focus where she can make the biggest impact. Similarly, when you delegate in your own organization, people can learn and contribute in new or different ways and will be more committed because they feel like an owner in the process. The company benefits because more gets done.

In my first year as an Air Force officer and a clinical laboratory manager, I did a lot of work to impress those around me. I felt like the more I did, the more I would impress my supervisor and my commanders. But I learned an important lesson; if I would take time to delegate responsibilities, my team benefited by learning, I got more done, my commanders were impressed with my leadership ability, and the entire organization became better. I always gave credit to the staff even though I could have easily assumed all the glory for myself. Ultimately, if something fails, I must hold myself responsible, but if it's a success, my team gets the glory. Giving responsibility to another does not in any way exempt you from the risk.

Remember, you are empowering other people to act on your behalf. You are still ultimately responsible when allowing someone to act as your representative. When you give your representative that responsibility, let them know that they are acting as your ambassador in this task. Give them clear, explicit instructions about their responsibility. You cannot expect to hold people responsible for tasks that you have not clearly defined or trained them for. Teddy Roosevelt once said, "The best executive is the one who has sense enough to pick good men to do what he wants done, and self-restraint enough to keep from meddling with them while they do." You don't need to get involved in the details of how they do it, but you still must give clear instructions as to what you want done.

Additionally, identify the outcome that you expect. For instance, you would tell your teammate that you need a project done, the expected time frame, and if it cannot be completed within the expected window, the reason for why it may not have been accomplished. Don't assume they know when it is due, tell them what you expect. Also, let them know if there is a reward for accomplishing the task/goal. For example, "If you meet production quotas, everyone gets a day off," or "If a project is completed ahead of time, I'll buy lunch."

When I delegate responsibility to one of my team, I give them a vision of what I expect, with the creative authority to make it their own. One time, I gathered some artists and asked them to paint a mural of a map. I told them my vision of how the map should look but let them add their creative ability. The outcome was a beautiful mural that was a showpiece for our facility.

Give Authority

I often see managers give people tasks but do not give them the authority to get it done. When you delegate work, think of authority as the gas that makes the car go. How much gas you put in the car will determine how far it will go. Sometimes, when you have new or inexperienced staff members, you'll only put in a few dollars of gas to get them started. As they progress and show their ability, you increase the amount of gas. Authority increases as responsibility is proven.

In an article, William Oncken, Jr., co-author of *The One Minute Manager Meets the Monkey*, said this about authority, "The concept of authority as something that causes another person to do what you want them to do is reflected in most definitions. For instance, the dictionary speaks of authority as, a power or right to direct the actions or thoughts of others usually because of rank or position, to issue commands and to punish for violations."[2] Again, the root idea seems to be controlling the actions of others. He goes on to talk about four elements of authority. "There is authority of competence, position, personality, and character. Your authority delegated to your staff will give them confidence. And as they succeed this will show your competence as a leader. The authority of position is purely, 'do it because I said so.' The authority of personality is evident in how people respond to your delegation of responsibility. Basically, they'll do it because they like you. But number one is the authority of your character. This is your credit rating. It lends to your integrity, honesty, loyalty, and ethics. If people respect the authority of your character, then when that authority is given to others they will carry out their responsibilities with the same character."[3]

I am not sure who coined the phrase, "exploration prior to delegation will bring self-determination," but I like it just the same. In my laboratory, I allowed my staff a certain level of authority to speak on my behalf. I told doctors that if they had a question, the technicians knew the answer. Prior to this, however, I had instructed my technicians so they knew their limits. If they needed to send tests out of our lab that would cost us money, I gave them a limit on the amount they could spend without my approval. When I was out of the office, the technician in charge knew how I would answer certain questions and the limits of what they could do. When I delegated responsibility to her, I gave her the authority to act on my behalf.

When you delegate responsibility, give enough authority so employees can get the work done, take initiative to make improvements, and keep things going when you are not there. Give your staff enough power to accomplish the objective. Many times, you must be willing to sacrifice your way of doing something in order to effectively delegate responsibility and authority to others.

Again, remember that when delegating authority and responsibility, you are ultimately held liable for the final outcome. Make sure you properly train your representative and discuss what their authority, and its limits, looks like. It's like signing a power of attorney. Remember the movie, *Rocky V*? When Rocky and Adrian returned from Russia, they found out they were broke. Rocky's brother-in-law, Paulie, had signed a blanket power of attorney giving their accountant all the authority to act on their behalf, who then took all their money.

One time, during my first two years in the Air Force, one of our patients needed some blood drawn for a test and was unable to come into the laboratory to have the procedure. I told the patient over the phone that I would come to their house, draw their blood, take it back to my laboratory, and run the test for them. The next day, I got in trouble for making that decision by myself, because I did not possess the responsibility nor authority. I learned a valuable lesson about delegation that day; you cannot delegate other people's responsibility or authority to yourself. In doing so, you create a liability for your supervisors.

On another occasion, I was filling in for my boss at an organizational meeting. The leader of the meeting asked someone in the facility to manage a new responsibility. I raised my hand and said that the people in my department were experts at that task and that we could probably manage it. Well, that meeting leader took that to mean I was nominating my boss for the role and assigned that responsibility to her the next day. I did not have authority to make that decision for our department, and my boss was, understandably, not too happy with me when she received her new assignment.

On the contrary, when I became a laboratory manager I instructed my team to take it upon themselves to do what was necessary for patient care. As long as it was legal and ethical, they didn't necessarily need my permission. In doing so, I gave them the authority and responsibility, but I still assumed the liability. I took a great risk in this, great trust if you will, but I felt it was necessary to empower my staff to learn, grow, and become responsible future leaders.

Ultimately, if your staff fails in the responsibilities that you've given them, ask yourself if you gave them enough authority and the right tools to complete the job. The measure of a leader is whether you have coached and trained your staff so well that you make yourself unnecessary.

Give Yourself a Break

There are significant benefits to delegating.

- Sharing responsibility lessens the load on the leader.
- Engaging others in decision-making or task responsibility makes the organization more successful.
- Sharing responsibilities makes for a happier work environment. If your employees are happier, you're happier. People tend to rise to the level of what is expected of them, especially if you share the responsibilities to meet the goal.
- Sharing responsibilities gives you the opportunity to increase your abilities in the executive and administrative functions that are necessary for your job. If you spend too much time doing tasks that should have been delegated, you risk fulfilling your primary responsibilities and growing in your role.

Effective leaders know they can achieve remarkable goals only if they delegate work to the good, able, and talented people around them. The logic is simple, incorporating more brains and bodies to tasks gets more things done within the same time frame. Taking tasks that are necessary, but do not require the leader's direct involvement, out of the leader's hands gives them time to concentrate on value-added jobs that fit their qualifications. The ability to delegate work is, therefore, a vital asset that all good leaders should have.

Other than improving your time management, effectively delegating work may decrease your stress and substantially improve your work life and overall health. Long-term mismanagement of stress affects your family, your free time, and even your health. In fact, an estimated 120,000 deaths a year are caused by workplace stress.[4] Nothing is more important than that.

Start assigning responsibility and authority today. How will you apply the lessons learned in this chapter?

_____

_____

_____

_____

_____

The price of success is hard work, dedication to the job at hand, and the determination that whether we win or lose, we have applied the best of ourselves to the task at hand.

The quality of a person's life is in direct proportion to their commitment to excellence, regardless of their chosen field of endeavor.

– Vince Lombardi

11

You're Set Up for the Set Up:
Perfect Practice Makes Perfect

Watching that volleyball match was a thing of extraordinary excitement. Each player performed as well as they could. Excellence was exhibited. The teamwork was evident. The hitters worked masterfully with precision and strength. Passes were just right, bumped at the perfect height and finesse. The setter placed the ball with speed and accuracy as if she were designed by God to do just that. I couldn't help but think, "This is how life should be. This is how work should be." Each player was set up for success by great coaching, teamwork, and excellence. Everyone knew their position, they knew their responsibility, and they carried out their task with precise execution. This is a culture of success.

Before he was the 20th President of the United States, James Garfield was the Principal of Hiram College in Ohio. The father of one of his students asked him if the course of study could be simplified so his son might be able to complete it by a shorter route. "Certainly," Garfield replied. "But, it all depends on what you want to make of your boy. When God wants to make an oak tree, He takes a hundred years. When He wants to make a squash, He requires only two months."[1]

Change and transition are difficult. Being better than yesterday takes effort. When you are in transition, don't fight it, cooperate with it. Fear fights; faith flows. Have faith in yourself, your team, and your ability. Change is about stretching, reaching for something that is just beyond your capability, ability, and strength. That's how you set up yourself and others for success.

John Wayne's gravestone is marked with the following inscription: "Tomorrow comes at midnight, very clean. It's perfect when it arrives and puts itself in our hands. It hopes we learned something from yesterday." The measure of success today is not whether you have a tough problem to deal with, but whether it's the same problem as yesterday.

The set up is not an overnight accomplishment. It's not a one-day event facilitated by a motivational speaker. It is the consistent practice of supporting others toward excellence. John Wooden, the eminently successful UCLA basketball coach, was asked his secret for producing stellar teams. He answered, "We master the basics. We drill over and over again on the fundamentals."[2]

One day, when I was in my early thirties, I was changing the spark plugs on my car. It wasn't a big job, but it was a necessary one. Once I was done, I started the engine to listen to how it ran and ensure each cylinder was firing correctly. As astonishing as it was to me, I did it right. I remembered when I was not so adept at such a mechanical endeavor. In my early twenties, while performing the same maintenance, I changed the spark plugs and started the engine, only to hear the sound of a rough idle. When I pushed the accelerator, the car jerked and would not move forward. I shut off the engine and checked the plugs, noticing that I had failed to insert one of them correctly, causing the car to misfire. I took the plug out, re-inserted it, and the car ran perfectly.

Your teams and organizations can work like a finely tuned engine if the right tools are in place and working as they should. **Each person should be in the right place at the right time doing the right things, a beautiful symphony of employees working together to accomplish the mission.**

Have you created the proper setting, or culture, to grow the right people, doing the right things, accomplishing success together? How do you measure this success? Is it how much money you have earned, a profit increase in your business, the number of friends or contacts you have, or your total followers on Instagram or Twitter? Amazon offers over 3,700 books that discuss how to measure success. There are also books about the science of success and how to measure success as an outcome. They all have the same general message: if you have reached your goals, you have success. The setting is perfect for the outcome it creates, good or bad.

When my daughter, Hannah, was sixteen, her volleyball coach explained her philosophy of the game to my wife and me. She was less concerned about whether the girls won each tournament. Rather, she was more concerned about how they played and how it would affect their chances for college recruitment. Yes, the girls also wanted to win and played their best to win each match, but they also cared more about their future. They wanted to continue to play the sport and have their education paid for through a scholarship. Together, the coach, the players, and the parents chose tournaments that gave the girls the most opportunity and exposure to college coaches and scouts. That was their measure of success and it paid off well. Several schools actively recruited my daughter and five of her teammates to play college volleyball for them.

When our laboratory staff wanted to win the Air Force laboratory team of the year award, we started with a series of small goals. First, we aligned our team around the larger goal. Did we want to work hard enough to win? Then we aligned our behavior to achieve those goals. What steps did we need to take to win? How did other teams in the past win? At the beginning of our fiscal year, we decided what we needed to finish each week, then each month. We marked each milestone as we accomplished it. Each person had individual goals to achieve so the team would have a complete, well-rounded award package. At the end, the team compiled our results report to compete at the highest level. We won our regional level award, which qualified us for the Air Force level award. We didn't win for the entire Air Force, but my team was pleased that we had done everything we could to set ourselves up for success.

Having read this book, you are now in a position to succeed. You are now in a position to be propelled in leadership, and that will take effort.

Many mornings when I am training for a running event or about to begin a strenuous workout, I watch a video about "The Grind." It motivates me and gets me ready for that run or workout. Some days, I may even listen when I am having a difficult time or need an extra boost of confidence. "You are a lion in a field of lions," it starts out. "All hunting the same elusive prey with the desperate starvation that says victory is the only thing that can keep you alive. So, believe that voice that says that you can run a little faster and you can throw a little harder, that for you, the laws of physics are merely a suggestion." "Luck is the last dying wish of those who want to believe that winning can happen by accident. Sweat, on the other hand, is for the ones who know it's a choice. So, decide now, because destiny waits for no one. When the time comes, and a thousand different voices are trying to tell you, 'You are not ready for it,' listen instead to that lone voice of descent, one that says, 'you are ready, you are prepared.' It's all up to you now."

Consider this: Information plus inspiration equals revelation. And revelation plus perspiration, multiplied by duration, equals celebration.

$I + In = R$ and $(R + P) \times D = C$

You have the material you need, and with the stories in this book combined with your own experiences, motivation, and goals, you have an opportunity for a revelation of what you can do and who you can be! It takes some work or perspiration, and it takes time, duration. Eventually, you will be celebrating success, accomplishment, and monumental achievements.

Too many people put more energy into avoiding the things that have caused them pain, rather than moving toward their destiny and vision. They avoid moving forward because of past failures or hurts. All that we do takes effort, determination, and grit. That takes moving beyond our excuses or fears.

No one can judge effort. Every day is a new opportunity to be better today than you were yesterday. You are different today than you were yesterday because you took time to read this. Now you are ready to implement what you've learned to propel yourself and your team to new and greater achievements.

You are ready to analyze the competition. You are ready to analyze your team, placing them in the right position, knowing their strengths. You will patiently wait for the right moment, seize it, and lead with confidence. At first, the growth and development may not be perfectly evident, just know that there is progress happening.

Zig Ziglar is attributed with a story about the Chinese bamboo tree. It's meant to be a reminder that outward progress doesn't necessarily reflect or measure inward progress. When the seed of the Chinese bamboo tree is planted, watered, and nurtured, it doesn't outwardly grow as much as an inch for years. There's no sign of growth. Not even a hint. The tree is carefully watered and fertilized each year, but nothing shows. So it goes, as the sun rises and sets for four years. The farmer and his wife have nothing tangible to show for their effort. After five years, the bamboo tree suddenly sprouts and grows eighty feet in just six weeks![3]

Did the little tree lie dormant for four years only to grow exponentially in the fifth? Or, was the little tree growing underground, developing a root system strong enough to support its potential for outward growth in the fifth year and beyond? Of course! Had the tree not developed a strong (but unseen) foundation, it could not have sustained its life as it grew.

As I bring this book to a close, I am traveling to my daughter, Bailey's, college graduation. She's the last of my children to achieve a degree. I am pondering her life and wondering if I did all I could to prepare her to be set up for her future. I think I did.

I taught her to develop patience by not intervening in some of her struggles. She saw my determination as I made it through working two jobs for many years while going to school, and yet I was still there to coach her soccer games. Because she's a foodie, her mom patiently taught her to cook so she could take care of herself, all the while instilling in her great value and pride, telling stories and pouring into her incredible wisdom.

Michelle and I created a setting that allowed her and our other children to be strong, independent people. We fostered a setting that allowed her to learn, grow, make mistakes, see correction, and develop the discipline to reach her goals. I certainly motivated her through those days of struggle in school and on the volleyball court and encouraged her to go for her master's degree.

She is a natural leader and has learned to analyze her surroundings and her competition. She has learned how to manage people at a retail business and has worked as an intern in a small rural hospital. She traveled to eight different countries during her four years of college, so she could become a more competent and cultured leader. She prepared. She learned and grew with great success. So, yes, I did *set* her *up*. She is ready.

And, so are you. Is it because you read these words? Maybe. More likely, it is because you wanted to be better, do more, and be more, so you grabbed this book to propel you toward that goal. You searched yourself, your heart, and said, "I can do this!"

Your dreams, no matter how big, are not in vain. Just because you don't see signs of progress now, do not grow weary in continuing to build toward your future; give it everything you have, heart and soul. You can't do this all by yourself. Why would you want to? Partner with others, delegate tasks, lead the charge, and encourage and motivate your people.

Obstinate people achieve success. While I was growing up, people used that word in a negative manner. I don't see it that way. It's a synonym for persistence. It's very definition is about staying the course. Don't change course to your dreams. Obstinate people are stubborn, so be stubborn in pursuit of your goals, your dreams, your future. Own your future. *Set up* your future.

Success is doing the very best you can, whether or not you become the best is not as important. No one principle or guideline of success describes the absolute necessities. Because of that, there are no complete, singularly reliable guarantees that if you do certain things, your desired result will happen. But, if you apply the principles and guidelines from this book, you exponentially increase your chances of success. **The measurable result of success is this: did you do what you set out to do?** If so, you have success. Did you grow as a leader? Did you grow the people around you? If so, you have success. Did you put the right people, in the right place, for the right purpose? If so, you have mastered the set up.

Acknowledgements

To my colleagues and friends, who have assisted in the production of this work - thank you!

Jackie Gaines – Mentor, leader, pioneer extraordinaire.

Lynne Cunningham – Insight and understanding that few possess.

Kris Ann Piazza – Resilient like none other and persistent to the end.

Rich Bluni – Inspired and encouraged by you each day.

Dr. Jeff Morris – Shalom my friend, brother, achi.

Paige Bindi – Our work made us friends, our kids made us crazy proud.

Colleen McCrory – Your ideas helped spur the success of this work.

Ted Riche – My brother from another mother; thank you for the laughs.

Stephanie Striepeck – Your keen details and support made me a better writer.

Jamie Stewart and Debbie Landers – Thank you for the opportunity to write what has been in my heart for 15 years.

Lindy Sikes – Your words became my words and made this work the very best it can be.

Lauren Westwood – Your creativity and inspiration make this work stand out.

Bill and Barb Cunningham – Sittin' on the dock of the bay(ou) watching dolphins roll away, being inspired. Thank you for your space.

And to all of my Studer Group colleagues and my military family: thank you for your service to caregiver, patient, and country.

References

Introduction:

1. CareerBuilder, "More Than One-Quarter of Managers Said They Weren't Ready to Lead When They Began Managing Others, Finds New CareerBuilder Survey," press release, March 28, 2011, http://www.careerbuilder.com/share/aboutus/press-releasesdetail.aspx?id=pr626&sd=3%2F28%2F2011&ed=12%2F31%2F2011.

2. Byford, Mark, Michael D. Watkins, and Lena Triantogiannis. "Onboarding Isn't Enough", *Harvard Business Review* May–June 2017 issue, https://hbr.org/2017/05/onboarding-isnt-enough.

Chapter 1:

1. Eker, T. Harv. *Secrets of the Millionaire Mind: Mastering the Inner Game of Wealth.* New York: Harper Business, 2005.

2. Sinek, Simon. "How Great Leaders Inspire Action." Filmed September 2009. TED video. https://www.ted.com/talks/simon_sinek_how_great_leaders_inspire_action.

3. Ibid

4. Zak, Paul J. "The Neuroscience of Trust." *Harvard Business Review*, January-February 2017 issue, https://hbr.org/2017/01/the-neuroscience-of-trust.

5. Ibid

6. Batterson. Mark. *Chase the Lion: If Your Dream Doesn't Scare You, It's Too Small.* New York: Crown Publishing Group, 2016.

7. *Merriam-Webster*, s.v. "set," accessed May 29, 2018, https://www.merriam-webster.com/dictionary/set.

Chapter 2:

1. Harter, Jim and Amy Adkins. "Employees Want a Lot More From Their Managers." *Harvard Business Review*, April 2, 2015, https://hbr.org/2015/04/what-great-managers-do-to-engage-employees.

2. Ibid

Chapter 3:

1. Goodman, John and Diane Ward. "Satisfied Patients Lower Risk and Improve the Bottom Line." *Patient Safety & Quality Healthcare*, March/April 2008 issue, https://www.psqh.com/analysis/satisfied-patients-lower-risk-and-improve-the-bottom-line.

2. Williams, Grace L. "Best Companies to Work for: Salesforce, Southwest Top Employee Satisfaction Survey." *Today*, May 5, 2016, https://www.today.com/money/best-companies-work-salesforce-southwest-top-employee-satisfaction-survey-t90741.

3. Martin, Emmie. "A Major Airline Says There's Something It Values More Than Its Customers, And There's A Good Reason Why." *Business Insider*, July 29, 2015, http://www.businessinsider.com/southwest-airlines-puts-employees-first-2015-7.

4. Sumers, Brian. "Why Wall Street Isn't Happy With Southwest's 43 Straight Years of Profits." *Skift*, August 16, 2016, https://skift.com/2016/08/16/why-wall-street-isnt-happy-with-southwests-43-straight-years-of-profits.

5. Sujansky, Joanne and Jan Ferri-Reed. *Keeping The Millennials: Why Companies Are Losing Billions in Turnover to This Generation – and What to Do About It.* New York: Wiley, 2009.

6. Abrashoff, Michael. *It's Your Ship: Management Techniques from the Best Damn Ship in the Navy.* New York: Grand Central Publishing, 2012.

7. Byford, Mark, Michael D. Watkins, and Lena Triantogiannis. "Onboarding Isn't Enough", *Harvard Business Review* May–June 2017 issue, https://hbr.org/2017/05/onboarding-isnt-enough.
8. Ibid
9. Ibid

Chapter 4:

1. Ericsson, K. Anders, Michael J. Prietula, and Edward T. Cokely. "The Making of an Expert." *Harvard Business Review*, July–August 2007 issue, https://hbr.org/2007/07/the-making-of-an-expert.
2. Ibid
3. Ibid

Chapter 5:

1. Hedges, Kristi. "8 Common Causes Of Workplace Demotivation." *Forbes*, January 20, 2014, https://www.forbes.com/sites/work-in-progress/2014/01/20/8-common-causes-of-workplace-demotivation/#a5a159442c6d.
2. Merriam-Webster, s.v. "motivation," accessed May 29, 2018, https://www.merriam-webster.com/dictionary/motivation.
3. *Wikipedia*, s.v. "motivation," last modified June 11, 2018, https://en.wikipedia.org/wiki/Motivation.
4. Warmth (user). "The True 7 Wonders of the World." *Stories of Kindness from Around the World* (blog). https://www.kindspring.org/story/view.php?sid=10090.
5. Carnegie, Dale. *How to Win Friends and Influence People*. New York: Simon & Schuster, 1936.
6. Ibid
7. Merriam-Webster, s.v. "invest," accessed May 29, 2018, https://www.merriam-webster.com/dictionary/invest.
8. Baldoni, John. "How Leaders Can Instill Pride and Purpose in the Workplace." *American Management Association* (blog). http://www.amanet.org/training/articles/how-leaders-can-instill-pride-of-purpose.aspx.

Chapter 6:

1. Whelchel, Hugh. "Fear of A Meaningless Life." *Institute for Faith, Work & Economics*, July 3, 2012, https://tifwe.org/fear-of-a-meaningless-life.

Chapter 7:

1. Anecdote from https://bible.org/illustration/oatmeal, citing Bits & Pieces (March 4, 1993): 23.
2. Anecdote from https://bible.org/illustration/three-kids-bragging-about-fathers.
3. McGhee, Paul E. *Health, Healing and The Amuse System: Humor As Survival Training*. Dubuque: Kendall Hunt Publishing, 1999.
4. Korobkin, Debra. "Humor in the Classroom: Considerations and Strategies." *College Teaching* 36, no. 4 (1988): 154-58. http://www.jstor.org/stable/27558304.
5. Ibid
6. Ibid
7. Zenger, Jack. "Workplace Feedback" Tis Better to Receive Than to Give." *Forbes*, April 19, 2012, https://www.forbes.com/sites/jackzenger/2012/04/19/workplace-feedbacktis-better-to-receive-than-to-give.
8. Ibid

Chapter 8:

1. Helmenstine, Anne Marie. "10 Interesting DNA Facts." *ThoughtCo.*, October 23, 2017, https://www.thoughtco.com/interesting-dna-facts-608188.
2. Ibid
3. Judge, Timothy, Joyce E. Bono, Remus Iles, and Megan W. Gerhardt. "Personality and Leadership: A Qualitative and Quantitative Review." *Journal of Applied Psychology* 87 no. 4, (2002): 765-780. doi: 10.1037//0021-9010.87.4.765.
4. Judge, Timothy A., Amy E. Colbert, and Remus Ilies. "Intelligence and Leadership: A Quantitative Review and Test of Theoretical Propositions." *Journal of Applied Psychology* 89 no. 3, (2004): 542-552. doi: 10.1037/0021-9010.89.3.542.
5. Judge, Timothy A., Ronald F. Piccolo, and Tomek Kosalka. "The Bright and Dark Sides of Leader Traits: A Review and Theoretical Extension of The Leader Trait Paradigm." *The Leadership Quarterly* 20 (2009): 855–875. doi: 10.1016/j.leaqua.2009.09.004.
6. DeMaio, Steven. "How to Identify Your Employees' Hidden Talents." *Harvard Business Review*, June 24, 2009, https://hbr.org/2009/06/how-to-identify-your-employees.

Chapter 9:

1. *Collins Dictionary*, s.v. "patience," accessed May 29, 2018, https://www.collinsdictionary.com/us/dictionary/english/patience.

2. *Merriam-Webster*, s.v. "perseverance," accessed May 29, 2018, https://www.merriam-webster.com/dictionary/perseverance.

3. Mejia, Zameena. "This Simple Speaking Trick Can Make You More Influential at Work." *CNBC*, July 19, 2017, https://www.cnbc.com/2017/07/18/pausing-before-you-speak-can-help-you-be-a-more-effective-communicator.html.

4. Ibid

5. Eurich, Tasha. "Discomfort Is What You Feel When You're Growing." *Entrepreneur*, October 16, 2015, https://www.entrepreneur.com/article/250126.

6. Roberts, Wess. *The Best Advice Ever for Leaders*. Kansas City: Andrews McMeel, 2002.

Chapter 10:

1. *Merriam-Webster*, s.v. "trust," accessed May 29, 2018, https://www.merriam-webster.com/dictionary/trust.

2. Blanchard, Ken, Bill Oncken, and Hal Burrows. "Monkey Business" *National Business News* 2 no. 4 (1990): 7.

3. Ibid

4. Blanding, Michael. "National Health Costs Could Decrease if Managers Reduce Work Stress." *Working Knowledge*, January 26, 2015, https://hbswk.hbs.edu/item/national-health-costs-could-decrease-if-managers-reduce-work-stress.

Chapter 11:

1. Anecdote from http://www.family-times.net/illustration/Success/200023.

2. Maxwell, John C. "Why John Wooden's Teams Won." *Success*, March 17, 2017, https://www.success.com/article/john-c-maxwell-why-john-woodens-teams-won.

3. Koh, Me Ra. "The Chinese Bamboo Tree: Looking for Growth." *Me Ra Koh* (blog). https://www.merakoh.com/artist-living/business-survival-tips/the-chinese-bamboo-tree-looking-for-growth.

Additional Resources

About Huron:

Huron is a global consultancy that helps our clients drive growth, enhance performance, and sustain leadership in the markets they serve. We partner with them to develop strategies and implement solutions that enable the transformative change our clients need to own their future.

Learn more at www.huronconsultinggroup.com.

About Studer Group, a Huron solution:

A recipient of the 2010 Malcolm Baldrige National Quality Award, Studer Group is an outcomes-based healthcare performance improvement firm that partners with healthcare organizations in the United States, Canada, and beyond, teaching them how to achieve, sustain, and accelerate exceptional clinical, operational, and financial results.

Working with Huron, we help to get the foundation right so organizations can build a sustainable culture that promotes accountability, fosters innovation, and consistently delivers a great patient experience and the best quality outcomes over time.

To learn more about Studer Group, visit www.studergroup.com or call 850-439-5839.

Coaching:

Studer Group coaches work with healthcare leaders to create an aligned culture accountable to achieving outcomes together. Working side-by-side, we help to establish, accelerate, and hardwire the necessary changes to create a culture of excellence. This leads to better transparency, higher accountability, and the ability to target and execute specific, objective results that organizations want to achieve.

Studer Group offers coaching based on organizational needs: Evidence-Based Leadership^{SM}, Health System, Emergency Department, Medical Group, and Rural Healthcare.

Learn more about Studer Group coaching by visiting www.studergroup.com/coaching.

Conferences:

Huron and Studer Group offer interactive learning events throughout the year that provide a fresh perspective from industry-leading keynote speakers and focused sessions that share evidence-based methods to improve consistency, reduce variance, increase engagement, and create highly profitable organizations. They also provide networking opportunities with colleagues and experts and help participants learn new competencies needed to continuously improve the quality and experience of patient-centered care.

Most learning events offer continuing education credits. Find out more about upcoming conferences and register at www.studergroup.com/conferences.

Speaking:

From large association events to exclusive executive training, Studer Group speakers deliver the perfect balance of inspiration and education for every audience.

As experienced clinicians and administrators, each speaker has a unique journey to share filled with expertise on a variety of healthcare topics. This personal touch along with hard-hitting healthcare improvement tactics empower your team to take action.

Learn more about Studer Group speakers by visiting www.studergroup.com/speaking.

Publishing:

Studer Group offers tactical, purpose-driven books that help healthcare professionals develop the skills they need to improve and sustain results across their organizations. For over 15 years, our resources have addressed industry challenges, elevate care delivery, and provide solutions for quality patient experience.

With more than 900,000 publications in circulation across the United States, Canada, Australia, New Zealand, China, and Japan, we are a trusted source for proven tactics and tools to help improve employee engagement, build leadership skills, and improve channels of communication.

Explore our catalog of resources by visiting www.publishing.studergroup.com.

Additional Offerings:

Healthcare leaders are facing unprecedented pressures that require changing care initiatives, payment models and caregiver evaluations. Balancing these challenges as leaders address patient expectations of improved and on-demand access to quality care at a better price can seem daunting. That's why Studer Group created innovative solutions to help organizations anticipate and manage these pressures, so leaders can successfully own their future rather than being disrupted by it. From CXO Development Institutes to Care Transition Intensives to High Reliability Programs to Perioperative Services to Post-Acute offerings, Studer Group experts will work side-by-side to plan and execute.

View all of our offerings at www.studergroup.com.

About the Author

Mark Noon is a national speaker at Studer Group, a Huron solution. His expertise includes employee engagement, leadership development, inspirational and motivational speaking, teamwork and creating value and bridging generational gaps in healthcare.

Mark has excelled in military and civilian healthcare leadership for more than 25 years. Spending his early military days as a lab technician, Mark received a commission as an officer and an immediate promotion to a lab management role. Mark served as clinical lab director for 12 and a half years before retiring as a major in the U.S. Air Force. Nine different assignments, seven states and a tour of duty in the Middle East created experiences few in healthcare or leadership ever acquire. Following his military retirement, Mark brought his operational and service excellence expertise to Studer Group. That experience shaped Mark's career-long commitment to developing skilled leaders.

He is an expert at conveying the value connection—driving results by teaching leaders to cultivate value in the people they manage. He has taught the highest level of civilian and military medical leaders about improving employee engagement and patient experience, Rounding for Outcomes and using Key Words at Key Times. Mark specializes in leading "kick-off" Leadership Development Institutes (LDIs), providing an exceptional foundational understanding of the Evidence-Based Leadership[SM] (EBL) Framework. Known for his energetic, affable presentation style, Mark easily connects with diverse audiences by creating a positive environment where people are ready to learn.

Mark lives in a small beach community near Destin, Florida with his wife, Michelle, and is the proud father of four children: Taylor, Hannah, Bailey, and Keenan.

How to Order Additional Copies of

Set Up:
Timeless Leadership Skills for Your Success

Online:
www.publishing.studergroup.com/set-up

By phone: 866-354-3473

By mail:
Studer Group
350 W. Cedar Street, Suite 300
Pensacola, FL 32502

Share this book with your team—and save!
If purchasing for a team, please contact us at 866-354-3473
to learn more about volume savings.

To learn more about Mark Noon and how you can
bring him to speak at your organization, visit
www.studergroup.com/people/mark-noon.